MARX'S
CAPITAL

MARX'S CAPITAL

Fourth Edition

Ben Fine and Alfredo Saad-Filho

Viva Books

New Delhi | Mumbai | Chennai | Kolkata | Bangalore | Hyderabad | Kochi | Guwahati

First Indian Edition 2007
Reprinted 2010

VIVA BOOKS PRIVATE LIMITED

- 4737/23 Ansari Road, Daryaganj, New Delhi 110 002
  E-mail: vivadelhi@vivagroupindia.net, Tel. 42242200
- 76, Service Industries, Shirvane, Sector 1, Nerul, Navi Mumbai 400 706
  E-mail: vivamumbai@vivagroupindia.net, Tel. 27721273, 27721274
- Jamals Fazal Chambers, 26 Greams Road, Chennai 600 006
  E-mail: vivachennai@vivagroupindia.net, Tel. 28290304, 28294241
- B-103, Jindal Towers, 21/1A/3 Darga Road, Kolkata 700 017
  E-mail: vivakolkata@vivagroupindia.net, Tel. 22836381, 22816713
- 7, Sovereign Park Apartments, 56-58, K. R. Road, Basavanagudi, Bangalore 560 004
  E-mail: vivabangalore@vivagroupindia.net, Tel. 26607409, 26607410
- 101-102 Mughal Marc Apartments, 3-4-637 to 641, Narayanguda, Hyderabad 500 029
  E-mail: vivahyderabad@vivagroupindia.net, Tel. 27564481, 27564482
- First Floor, Beevi Towers, SRM Road, Kaloor, Kochi 682 018, Kerala
  E-mail: vivakochi@vivagroupindia.net, Tel: 0484-2403055, 2403056
- 232, GNB Road, Beside UCO Bank, Silpukhuri, Guwahati 781 003
  E-mail: vivaguwahati@vivagroupindia.net, Tel: 0361-2666386

Published by arrangement with

Pluto Press
345, Archway Road,
London N6 5AA

ISBN: 978-81-309-0620-1

Published by Vinod Vasishtha for Viva Books Private Limited, 4737/23, Ansari Road, New Delhi 110 002. Printed and bound by Anand Sons, Delhi - 110 092.

The best points in my book are: (1) the *double character of labour*, according to whether it is expressed in use value or exchange value ... (2) the treatment of *surplus value independently of its particular* forms as profit, interest, ground rent, etc.

Marx to Engels, *Selected Correspondence*, Letter 99, Lawrence & Wishart, London, 1934.

no credit is due to me for discovering the existence of classes in modern society or the struggle between them. Long before the bourgeois historians had described the historical development of this class struggle and bourgeois economists the economic anatomy of the classes. What I did that was new was to prove: (1) that the *existence of classes* is only bound up with *particular historical phases in the development of production*, (2) that the class struggle necessarily leads to *the dictatorship of the proletariat*, (3) that this dictatorship itself only constitutes the transition to the *abolition of all classes* and to a *classless society.*

Marx to J. Weydemeyer, *Selected Works of Marx and Engels*, Lawrence & Wishart, London, 1968, p. 679.

CONTENTS

Acknowledgements xi
Preface to the Fourth Edition xiii

1 History and Method 1
Marx's Philosophy 1
Method 5
Marx's Economics 9
Issues and Further Reading 12

2 Commodity Production 14
The Labour Theory of Value 15
Labour and Labour Power 22
The Fetishism of Commodities 25
Issues and Further Reading 29

3 Capital and Exploitation 31
Exchange 31
Capital 33
Surplus Value and Exploitation 36
Absolute and Relative Surplus Value 40
Machinery and Technical Change 44
Productive and Unproductive Labour 46
Issues and Further Reading 48

4 **The Circuit of Industrial Capital** 51
The Money Circuit of Capital 51
The Circuit as a Whole 53
Issues and Further Reading 59

5 **Economic Reproduction** 61
Simple Reproduction 61
Expanded Reproduction 63
Social Reproduction 70
Issues and Further Reading 72

6 **Accumulation of Capital** 74
Primitive Accumulation 74
The Development of Capitalist Production 79
Competition and Capital Accumulation 82
Issues and Further Reading 87

7 **Capitalism and Crisis** 89
Marx's Theory of Accumulation and Crisis 89
Possibilities of Crisis 91
Accumulation, Crisis and the Development of the Proletariat 96
Issues and Further Reading 100

8 **The Compositions of Capital** 102
The Technical Composition of Capital 102
The Organic and Value Compositions 104
Issues and Further Reading 108

9 **The Falling Rate of Profit** 109
Summary of the Argument 110

The Law as Such and the Counteracting Tendencies 111
The Internal Contradictions of the Law 114
The Empirical Implications of the Law 116
LTRPF and Crisis Theory 118
A Response to Okishio 121
Issues and Further Reading 125

10 **The Transformation Problem** 126
From Values to Prices of Production 127
Marx's Transformation and Its Critics 130
Issues and Further Reading 134

11 **Merchant's Capital** 135
Marx's Category of Merchant's Capital 135
Modified Prices of Production 137
Merchant's Capital at a More Complex Level 139
Issues and Further Reading 141

12 **Banking Capital and the Theory of Interest** 142
Interest-Bearing Capital 143
Money Capital and the Financial System 144
Interest as an Economic Category 148
Issues and Further Reading 152

13 **Marx's Theory of Agricultural Rent** 153
Differential Rent 1 155
Differential Rent 2 157
Absolute Rent 160
Issues and Further Reading 164

14 Conclusion: Marxism and the Twenty-First Century 166
Class 167
The State and Globalisation 171
Capital's Environment 174
Socialism 176
Issues and Further Reading 180

References 182
Index 191

ACKNOWLEDGEMENTS

This book was initially prepared in the early 1970s from courses given at Birkbeck College, University of London, on 'Marxist Economics' and 'The Distribution of Income and Wealth'. Thanks to those who taught and attended those courses. Bob Rae and Simon Mohun read earlier versions of the first edition and made many suggestions that were incorporated. Since then many have contributed to the improvement of the text through the subsequent editions.

Alfredo Saad-Filho is grateful to Rita and Kamayuri for their support during the preparation of this manuscript.

PREFACE TO THE FOURTH EDITION

Marx's Capital was originally written in the early 1970s and was very much a product of its time. Then, in Britain and elsewhere, an interest in Marx's political economy was awakened after several years of intense repression under the guise of the 'cold war'. This interest grew, and was fed by the left-wing movements sweeping across the world, the evident decline of the world capitalist economy, and the rejection of traditional theory's explanations of the collapse of the post-war 'boom'. Much has changed since then, and successive editions of this book have, in their own way, reflected the shifting fortunes of political economy.

It is years since the previous edition was published, but the reason for launching this fourth edition runs deeper than the exhaustion of old stock. It anticipates, and hopefully in its own way contributes to, a revival of political economy in general and of Marxist political economy in particular. Such optimism is based on a number of factors.

First, while mainstream economics has tightened its intolerant grip on the discipline, dismissing heterodoxy as failing the tests of mathematical and statistical rigour, there are increasing signs of dissatisfaction with the orthodoxy. There is a growing search for alternatives among those studying economics and the other social sciences.

Second, following the predominance of post-modernism and neoliberalism in setting intellectual agendas across the social sciences over the past two decades, there is now a reaction against the extremes of their worst excesses in theory and practice. Critical thought has turned towards understanding the nature of contemporary capitalism, as most notably reflected in the rise of concepts such as globalisation and social capital over the past decade. Inevitably, the result is to raise the question of the economy outside of the discipline of economics itself, and to seek guidance from political economy.

Third, the long period of relative stagnation following the breakdown of the post-war boom, and the rise of post-modernism and neoliberalism, have had the paradoxical effect of allowing the capitalist economy to be perceived as engaging in business as usual even if on a sluggish basis. The eruption of financial crises over the past decade has shattered this perspective and brought to the fore the particularly prominent role being played by finance. The systemic relations between finance and industry, or the rest of the economy more generally, should occupy a prominent place in the subject matter of political economy.

Fourth, material developments have also promoted the case for political economy. These include: the growing realisation that environmental degradation, most notably through global warming, is intimately related to capitalism; the collapse of the Soviet Union but the recognition that capitalism has not furnished a progressive alternative even on its own narrow terms; and the eruption of what appear to be most conveniently described as imperial wars even if fought under the name of anti-terrorism or provision of human rights.

Last, if by no means least, the TINA (there is no alternative) of neoliberalism has now become countered by the TINOA (there is no other alternative) of the so-called Third Way. While still a magnet for those who seek a reformist politics within the confines of capitalism, Third Wayism is already tarnished in ideology and in deed. The case for socialism needs to be made as never before, and it rests upon political economy both for its critique of capitalism and for the light it sheds on the potential for alternatives.

Each of these issues is newly addressed to a greater or lesser extent in this new edition. But the main purpose of this book remains to provide as simple and concise an exposition of Marx's political economy as the complexity of his ideas allows. Because it is constrained to be short the arguments are condensed but remain simple; nevertheless, some of the material will require careful reading, particularly the later chapters. Not surprisingly, the text has increased in size, doubling from its original length of 25,000 words, as new topics have been added, drawn both from Marx's own political economy and its contemporary relevance. Other additions include chapter-by-chapter highlighting of controversies, issues for debate and corresponding further readings, which will offer guidance to those interested in more scholarly texts. It is with regret that this has led to the current edition losing much of the simplicity of the previous ones but, for ease of reading, footnotes and references have again been omitted. This (hopefully minor) difficulty is perhaps compounded by the occasional references to how Marx's political economy differs from orthodox economics, placing some strain on the non-economist. But, hopefully, such difficulties can be overlooked where necessary and, otherwise, offer compensating insights.

For the fourth edition, I have been joined by Alfredo Saad-Filho as co-author. This has been in order to refresh the text that remains from earlier editions and to add refreshing new text drawing on Alfredo's significant contribution to value theory. We have maintained a close intellectual relationship for many years, developing a mutual and common understanding of Marx's political economy as is reflected in this new edition of the book. We would like to thank and to encourage those who continue to study and teach Marxist economics seriously, during a period when it has been extraordinarily hard to do so.

Ben Fine
July 2003

1
History and Method

Throughout his adult life Marx pursued the revolutionary transformation of capitalist society, most famously through his writings, but also through agitation and organisation of the working class – Marx was, for example, one of the leaders of the First International Working Men's Association between 1864 and 1876. In his written works, Marx attempts to uncover the general process of historical change, to apply this understanding to particular types of societies, and to make concrete studies of specific historical situations. This chapter briefly reviews Marx's intellectual development and the main features of his method. The remainder of this book analyses in further detail other aspects of his work, especially those to be found in the three volumes of *Capital*, his leading work of political economy.

Marx's Philosophy

Karl Marx was born in Germany in 1818 and began an early university career studying law. His interest quickly turned to philosophy, which, at that time, was dominated by Hegel and his disciples. They were idealists, believing that theoretical concepts can legitimately be developed more or less independently of material reality. For the

Hegelians, reality is the outcome of an evolving system of concepts, or movement towards the 'Absolute Idea', with a structure of concepts connecting the relatively abstract to the increasingly concrete. The Hegelians believed that intellectual progress explains the advance of government, culture and the other forms of social life. Therefore, the study of consciousness is the key to the understanding of society, and history is a dramatic stage on which institutions and ideas battle for hegemony. In this ever-present conflict, each stage of development contains the seeds of its own transformation into a higher stage. Each stage is an advance on those that have preceded it, but it absorbs and transforms elements from them. This process of change, in which new ideas do not so much defeat the old as resolve conflicts or contradictions within them, Hegel called the *dialectic.*

Hegel died in 1831. When Marx was still a young man at university, two opposing groups of Hegelians, Young (radical) and Old (reactionary), both claimed to be Hegel's legitimate successors. The Old Hegelians believed that Prussian absolute monarchy, religion and society represented the triumphant achievement of the Idea in its dialectical progress. In contrast the Young Hegelians, dangerously anti-religious, believed that intellectual development had far to advance. This set the stage for a battle between the two schools, each side believing a victory heralded the progress of German society. Having observed the absurdity, poverty and degradation of much of German life, Marx identified himself initially with the Young Hegelians.

However, Marx's sympathy for the Young Hegelians was extremely short-lived, largely because of the influence on him of Feuerbach, who was a materialist. This does not mean that Feuerbach was crudely interested in his own welfare – in fact, his dissenting views cost him his academic career. He believed that far from human consciousness dominating life and existence, it was human needs that determined consciousness. In *The Essence of Christianity* Feuerbach mounted a simple but brilliant polemic against religion. Humans needed God because religion satisfied an emotional need. To satisfy this need, humans had projected their best qualities on to a God figure, worshipping what had been made to the extent that God had assumed an independent existence in human consciousness. To regain their humanity, people need to substitute the love of each other for the love of God.

Marx was immediately struck by this insight. Initially he criticised Feuerbach for seeing people as individuals struggling to fulfil a given 'human nature', rather than as social beings. However, he soon moved beyond Feuerbach's materialism. He did this in two ways. First, he extended Feuerbach's materialist philosophy to all dominant ideas prevailing in society, beyond religion to ideology and people's conception of society as a whole. Second, he extended Feuerbach's ideas to history. Feuerbach's analysis had been entirely ahistorical and non-dialectical: humans satisfy an emotional need through religion, but the origin of that need remains unexplained and unchanging whether satisfied by God or not. Marx sees the solution to this problem in material conditions. Human consciousness is critical in Marx's thought, but it can only be understood in relation to historical, social and material circumstances. In this way, Marx establishes a close relationship between dialectics and history, which would become a cornerstone of his own method. Consciousness is primarily determined by material conditions but these themselves evolve dialectically through human history.

Whether in the minds of Hegel, his various disciples and critics, or Marx, this account reveals a common property in their thought – that things do not always immediately appear as they are. For Feuerbach, for example, God does not exist other than in the mind but appears to do so to satisfy a human need. Under capitalism, a free labour market conceals exploitation, and political democracy suggests equality rather than continuing privilege and power. This divorce between reality (or content or essence) and the way it appears (or form) is a central aspect of Marx's (dialectical) thought. It forges the link between abstract concepts (such as class and value for example) and their concrete and practical presence in everyday life (through wages, prices and profits).

The task that Marx sets himself, primarily for capitalism, and which he recognises as extremely demanding with, in his own words, no royal road to science, is to trace the connection and the contradictions between the abstract and the concrete. It involves adopting an appropriate method, a judicious starting point in choice of the abstract concepts, and a careful unfolding of their historical and logical content to reveal the relationship between the way things are and the way they appear to be.

Significantly, as will be clear from Marx's discussion of commodity fetishism (in chapter 2), appearances are not necessarily simply false or illusory as in religious beliefs. For we cannot wish away wages, profits and prices simply because we recognise them to be the form in which capitalism organises exploitation. In this case, the appearances are part and parcel of reality itself, both representing and concealing more fundamental aspects of capitalism that an appropriate dialectics is designed to reveal. How is this complexity to be unravelled?

Method

In contrast with his extensive writings on political economy, history, anthropology, current affairs and much else, Marx never wrote a detailed essay on his own method. This is because his work is primarily a critique of capitalism and its apologists, in which methodology plays an important but secondary role, and is generally submerged within other arguments. Moreover, Marx's method cannot be summarised into a set of universal rules; specific applications of his materialist dialectics should be developed in order to address each problem. The best-known example of the application of Marx's method is his critical examination of capitalism in *Capital*. In this work, Marx's approach has five important broad features. These will be added to and refined, often implicitly, throughout the text.

First, social phenomena exist, and can be understood, only in their historical context. Trans-historical generalisations, supposedly valid everywhere and for all time, are normally either vacuous, or invalid, or both. Human societies are immensely flexible. They can be organised in profoundly different ways, and only detailed analysis can offer valid insights about their internal structure, contradictions, changes and limits. In particular, Marx considers that societies are distinguished by the mode of *production* under which they are organised, feudalism as opposed to capitalism for example. Each mode of production is structured according to its class relations, for which there are appropriate corresponding categories of analysis. Just as a wage labourer is not a serf who happens to be paid or a 'free slave', so a capitalist is not a feudal baron receiving profit in place of tribute. Societies are distinguished by the modes of production under which they are organised and so must be the concepts used to understand them.

Second, then, theory loses its validity if pushed beyond its historical and social limits. This is a consequence of the need for concepts to be drawn out from the societies they are designed to address. For example, Marx claims that in capitalism the workers are exploited because they produce more value than they appropriate through their wage (see chapter 3); this gives rise to surplus value. This conclusion, and the corresponding notion of surplus value, are valid only for capitalist societies. It may shed some light on exploitation in other societies, but the modes of exploitation and the roots of social and economic change in these societies must be sought afresh – analysis of capitalism, even if correct, does not automatically provide the principles by which to understand how other societies are structured.

Third, Marx's analysis is internally structured by the relationship between theory and history. In contrast with Hegelian idealism, Marx's method is not centred upon conceptual derivations. For him, purely conceptual reasoning is limited because it is impossible to explain why the relations evolving in the analyst's head must also hold in the real world. More generally, idealism errs because it seeks to explain reality primarily through conceptual advance, even though reality exists only historically and materially outside of the thinking head. Jokingly, Marx suggested that the Young Hegelians would be able to abolish the laws of gravity if they could just escape from believing in them! In contrast, Marx recognises that reality is shaped by social structure and tendencies and counter-tendencies (which can be derived dialectically), as well as by unpredictable contingencies (which cannot be so derived). The outcomes of their interactions cannot be determined in advance. Consequently, although materialist dialectics can help understand both the past and the present, it is impossible to foretell the future (Marx's analysis of the law of the tendency of the rate of profit to fall and the counter-tendencies is a telling example of this approach, see chapter 9). Marx's recognition that historical analysis belongs within the method of study (history and logic are inseparable) is not a concession to empiricism; it merely acknowledges the fact that a shifting reality cannot be reduced to, let alone determined by, a system of concepts.

Fourth, materialist dialectics identifies the key concepts, structures, relationships and levels of analysis required for the explanation of the concrete, or more complex and specific outcomes. In *Capital*, Marx employs materialist dialectics to pinpoint the essential features of capitalism and their contradictions, to explain the structure and dynamics of this mode of production, and to locate the potential sources of historical change. His study systematically brings out more complex and concrete concepts which help to reconstruct the realities of capitalism in thought. These concepts help to explain the historical development of capitalism, and indicate its critical vulnerabilities. In doing this, concepts at distinct levels of abstraction always co-exist in Marx's analysis. Theoretical progress includes the introduction of new concepts, the refinement and reproduction of the existing concepts at greater levels of concreteness and complexity, and the introduction of historical evidence in order to provide a richer and more determinate account of reality.

Fifth, Marx's method focuses upon historical change. In the *Communist Manifesto*, the preface to the *Contribution to the Critique of Political Economy* and the introduction to the *Grundrisse*, Marx famously summarises his account of the relationship between structures of production, social relations and historical change. Marx's views have often been interpreted mechanically, as if the supposedly unilinear development of technology unproblematically guides historical change – in which case social change is determined by the development of production. This interpretation of Marx is invalid. There is a relationship of mutual determination between technology, society and history (and other factors) but in ways that are invariably influenced by the mode of social organisation. For example, under capitalism technological development is primarily driven by the profit imperative across all commercial activity. Under feudalism, the production of luxury goods and (military) services and, to a certain extent, agricultural implements is paramount which, in the absence of the profit motive, limits the scope and pace of technical advance. In contrast, Marx argues that in communist societies technological development would seek to eliminate repetitive, physically demanding, unsafe and unhealthy tasks, reduce overall labour time, satisfy basic needs and develop human potential (see chapter 14).

In 1845–46 when he was writing *The German Ideology* with Engels and the *Theses on Feuerbach*, Marx had already begun to be influenced by the ideas of the French socialists. Their ideas cannot be discussed here in detail. Suffice it to say that they were fostered by the radical heritage of the French Revolution and the failure of the emerging bourgeois society to realise the demands of *'liberté, égalité et fraternité'*. The French socialists were also deeply involved in class politics, and many believed in the necessity and possibility of revolutionary seizure of power by the workers.

Marx's synthesis between German philosophy and French socialism would have remained incomplete without his critique of British political economy, which he studied later. Given his conceptions of philosophy and history, explained above, it was natural for Marx to turn his study to economics in order to understand contemporary capitalist society, and identify its strengths and limitations, and its potential for transformation into a socialist (communist) society. To do this he immersed himself in British political economy, in particular developing the labour theory of value from the writings of Adam Smith and, especially, David Ricardo. For Marx, it is insufficient to base the source of value on labour time of production, as Ricardo presumes. For Ricardo's view takes for granted the existence of exchange, prices and commodities. That commodities are more valuable because they embody more labour begs the question of why there are commodities at all, let alone whether it is a relevant abstraction to assume that they exchange at their labour time of production. This anticipates the next chapter, but it illustrates a key feature of Marx's method and a common criticism by Marx of other writers. Marx finds other economists not only wrong in content but also inadequate in intent. What economists tend to assume as timeless features of humans and societies, Marx was determined to root out and understand in historical context.

Marx does take for granted the need (for society) to work in order to produce and consume. However, the way in which production is organised has to be revealed, and the dependence of other social relations on this needs to be explained both structurally and historically. Very briefly, Marx argues that when working – producing the material conditions for their individual and social reproduction – people enter into definite social relations with each other, as slave or master, lord or serf, capitalist or wage earner, and so on. Patterns of life are determined by existing social conditions, in particular the places to be filled in the process of production. These relations exist independently of individual choice, even though they have been established in the course of the historical development of society.

The social relations of production specific to a particular mode of production (feudalism, capitalism, and so on) are best studied as class relations in all but the simplest societies. They are the basis on which the society is constructed. Just as freedom to buy and sell is a key legal characteristic of capitalist society, so divine or feudal obligations are the legal foundations of feudalism. In addition, self-justifying political, legal, intellectual and distributional forms are also established, and these in general blinker and discourage all but the most conventional views of society, whether by force of habit or otherwise. The serf feels bound by loyalty to master and king, and any vacillation can be punished severely. The wage earner has both freedom and compulsion to sell labour power. There can be struggle for higher wages, but this does not question the wage system. In contrast, probing into the *nature* of capitalism is frowned upon by the authorities. Whereas individual dissent is often tolerated, anti-capitalist mass movements are invariably repressed.

In this context, Marx castigates the Classical political economists and the utilitarians for assuming that certain characteristics of human behaviour, like greed, are permanent features of 'human nature' when, in reality, they are characteristics generated in individuals by particular societies. Consequently, they also take for granted those features of capitalist society that Marx felt it necessary to explain: the monopoly of the means of production by a small minority, the wage employment of the majority, the distribution of the products by monetary exchange, and remuneration involving the economic categories of prices, profits and wages.

Marx's value theory is a penetrating contribution to social science in that it concerns itself with the relations that people set between themselves, rather than the technical relationships between things or the art of economising. Marx is not interested primarily in constructing a price theory, a set of efficiency criteria or a series of welfare propositions; he never intended to be a narrow 'economist' or even a political economist. Marx was a critical social scientist, whose work straddles, and rejects, the barriers separating academic disciplines. The crucial questions for Marx concern the sources of stability and crises in capitalism, and how the will to change it can develop into successful transformative (revolutionary) activity. These questions remain valid into the twenty-first century.

Issues and Further Reading

Several biographies of Karl Marx are available; see, for example, David McLellan (1974) and Francis Wheen (2000). Marx's intellectual trajectory is reviewed by Allen Oakley (1983, 1984, 1985). The history of Marxian economics is surveyed by Michael Howard and John King (1989, 1991), and the key concepts in the Marxian literature are authoritatively explained in Tom Bottomore (1991). The history of dialectics is comprehensively reviewed by Simeon Scott (1999).

Marx rarely discusses his own method. The best-known exceptions are the introduction to Marx (1981a), the prefaces and postfaces to Marx (1976) and the preface to Marx (1987). Subsequent literature and controversy has more than made up for Marx's own apparent neglect. Almost every aspect of his method has been subject to close scrutiny and differing interpretations from supporters and critics alike. Our presentation here is embarrassingly simple and superficial in breadth and depth. It draws upon Ben Fine (1980, ch. 1 and 1982, ch. 1) and Alfredo Saad-Filho (2002, ch. 1), which should be consulted for a more comprehensive interpretation of Marx's method. Others have examined in considerable detail the role of class, modes of production, dialectics, history, the influence of other thinkers, and so on, in Marx's analysis. In the context of political economy, Chris Arthur has written extensively on Marx's method; see, for example, Arthur

(2002). See also Duncan Foley (1986, ch. 1) and Roman Rosdolsky (1977, part 1). For alternative views, drawing upon a Hegelian interpretation of Marx, see Fred Moseley (1993) and Tony Smith (1990). For a critique, see John Rosenthal (1997) and the ensuing debates in *Science & Society* (63 (3), 1999 and 64 (4), 2000). Mechanistic interpretations of Marx, suggesting rigid causal determination between class relations or the economic and other factors, for example, are criticised by Ellen Wood (1984).

2
Commodity Production

Marx is renowned for his commitment to what is taken to be *the* labour theory of value. Many different aspects of his analysis of value and capital(ism) have been the subject of fierce controversy, along the lines both of being for or against Marx and, closely related but distinct, over differing interpretations of what he really meant – commentators differ over what he is saying as well as over whether it is correct or not. As a result, there are many different interpretations of the labour theory of value, many of which are foisted upon Marx out of ignorance, a wish to dismiss him and, perversely, in seeking to defend him. Further, it is often possible to trace disputes over Marx's political economy back to differences over his value theory. Rightly or wrongly, two issues have been fundamental in these continuing debates – has Marx unduly privileged labour in some way by adopting the *labour* theory of value, and how well does the labour theory of value serve as a theory of prices?

The purpose of this chapter is to embark upon an analytical journey that is carried forward throughout the remainder of the book. It does so by asking very different questions of the labour theory of value, ones that are closer to the method and content of Marx's work. For him, the labour theory of value cannot be proven correct by some conceptual wizardry or through some technical or algebraic acrobatics. Rather, Marx's value theory is concerned self-consciously to reproduce in thought the economic relations, processes and structures that prevail in capitalist society (see chapter 1). It is against this test that his value theory, and interpretations of it, should be judged. While Marx's value theory has simple beginnings, which are the focus of this chapter, it becomes richer and more complicated as it unfolds to confront the complexities of capitalism itself. It will be shown in later chapters that these complexities, far from negating Marx's value theory as invalid, confirm its internal consistency and explanatory power.

The Labour Theory of Value

In analysing a mode of production, for example capitalism, Marx's starting point is always production – how do capitalist societies produce the material conditions of their own reproduction? In any society, production creates use values, that is to say useful things such as food, clothing and houses, as well as immaterial products like educational, health and other personal services, all of which are necessary for the continuing existence of the society. Thus, the division of labour and the production of use values can be taken for granted as enduring features of human organisation. But who produces what and how, and with what implications for the economy and society, are crucial questions across the social sciences. Different disciplines and ideologies have given different answers, ranging from pursuit of self-interest to the idea of necessity as the mother of invention. Mainstream (orthodox or neoclassical) economics, in particular, has taken the need for consumption as justifying a universal approach or method in which economics is the science concerned with the allocation of scarce resources to meet insatiable needs. From this viewpoint, the economy may be organised through the market, the state, the household or through slavery, for example. These are merely details as opposed to the fundamental scarcity–need duality that is the focus of mainstream economics, and which provides the yardstick with which to measure the relative efficiency of the alternatives.

By contrast, for Marx social, especially class, relations are essential in distinguishing one economy from another, as well as differences within an economy. This involves not only the property and distributional relations that define the modes of production, who owns what and why, but also how ownership is organised and gives rise to forms of control of labour and its products, as well as other aspects of social organisation. Thus, for example, a crucial feature of capitalism is that it is a highly developed system of *commodity* production. What is its significance? Following Adam Smith, Marx distinguishes use value from exchange value within each commodity: their usefulness, which cannot be quantified, from the ability to exchange with other commodities, which can be quantified. Every commodity has a use value, or ability to satisfy human needs, without which it could not be sold and, therefore, would not be produced. But not every use value is a commodity, for use values which are created naturally, that are freely available or are not exchanged for money on the marketplace have no exchange value (for example sunlight, air, open spaces, wild fruits, production for personal use or production for or on behalf of relatives or friends).

Exchange value embodies an equivalence relationship between objects. This relationship has to satisfy certain properties, which become familiar to us in daily life, especially in the marketplace and in commercial calculation however simple or complex. If x exchanges for y ($x \sim y$ say), then $2x \sim 2y$. If, in addition, $u \sim v$, then (u and x) $\sim$ (v and y), and so on. But there is an unlimited number of relationships satisfying these properties, for example, weight or volume. The question Marx seeks to answer is what social relationship can provide the basis for systematic (rather than fortuitous) market exchanges and, more generally, for social reproduction under specific historical circumstances? What is it that allows commodities to be equivalents in exchange? In the case of weight or volume, equivalence is due to physical or natural properties, namely mass and size, respectively, properties that exist irrespective of whether they are actually measured or not. Further, although every commodity is characterised by its particular physical properties that, in part, give it its use value (the other part being derived from the culture of consumption and use), its exchange value is unrelated to these properties. As mentioned already, the most useful things, air, sunlight and water, often have little or no exchange value. Nor did stone in the Stone Age as there was little or no exchange. What creates the relationship of exchange, then, is not a physical relationship between goods but a historically specific social one, not least the way in which the production of use values is organised – for the market. Mainstream economics has begun to take more notice of this recently by accepting that institutions or whatever matter for the efficacy of exchange, not least because markets are imperfect in some sense. But this is to get the argument the wrong way round. Before examining institutions as the response to the market, the market itself has to be explained (as an 'institution' or otherwise). At a deeper level, markets themselves are not simply some neutral mechanism of exchange but fundamentally reflect the social relations that underpin them.

This leads Marx to suggest that underlying the equivalence between commodities as use values is a qualitative and quantitative relationship between the producers of those commodities. This is because, for Marx, it is axiomatic that throughout history people have lived by their labour: if everyone stops working, no society can survive beyond a few days. Further, beyond the simplest societies, some have always lived without working, by the labour of others. However, this appropriation of one person's labour (or its products) by another takes different forms and is justified in different ways in different societies. Under feudalism, the products are often distributed by direct appropriation justified by feudal or even divine right. Under capitalism, the products of labour generally take the form of commodities, and they are distributed by free market exchanges. How this freedom brings about an appropriation of the labour of one class by another will be discussed in chapter 3. For the moment, we are only interested in the nature of the exchange relationship. In other words, in a commodity-producing society, what is special about production and labour?

To answer this question, Marx takes a bold and potentially controversial step. He defines commodities as being use values produced by labour for exchange. This means that not everything which is exchanged, even through the market, is a commodity. Perhaps this is readily acceptable in the case of bribery or even casually marketed second-hand goods, although each of these commands a price (i.e. takes the form of commodity) in its own way. But, in part to anticipate, for Marx, these are incidental phenomena, playing no essential role in social reproduction, and causally and analytically to be abstracted from in addressing commodity production in general and under capitalism in particular. It follows that a fundamental property which all commodities share in common is that they are the products of labour. By the same token, in commodity society concrete labours (producing specific use values) are connected with one another through the market, or through the exchange of their products for money.

This is a qualitative and impersonal social relationship, for example we generally buy commodities without knowing anything about who has produced them and how. For commodity production requires a division of labour within and across different workplaces, where different labours are contributed, brought together and measured against one another, albeit indirectly, through the market. This social process is the basis of the labour theory of value, and it embodies relationships that can easily be theoretically quantified by analysing exchange from the viewpoint of the labour time socially (rather than individually) necessary to produce commodities: for example, the amount of labour time required to bake a loaf of bread when contrasted with that required to sew a shirt (and, more importantly, how these labour times are determined and modified through technological and other changes). The labour theory of value is not a metaphysical notion, for it analytically captures the essential aspects of material life under capitalism, concerning how production is organised and attached to the market, and how the products of social labour are appropriated and distributed within society.

Marx realises that in capitalist societies, where products typically take the form of commodities, production is primarily for exchange for profit rather than immediate use. Capitalism is a system in which the aim of production is social use values – use values for others unknown because of the anonymity of the market. The production of social use values, market exchanges and profit-making are intimately linked to one another. But just as products embody social use values (production for persons unknown, reached through the market), so they are created by social labour in the abstract (by wage workers unknown, hired through the labour market and disciplined within competing firms by the profit imperative, and outside by the financial system and the stock market). In capitalist societies, the products of concrete labour count as abstract social labour. In this respect, exchange does not concern quality, or type of concrete labour, but only quantity of abstract labour, expressed through commodity prices. In exchange, what matters in how much you have to pay is not the use value you want – whether the labour time was expended by a baker, tailor, painter or computer programmer – but what amounts of abstract (socially necessary, rather than individual and concrete) labour time have been expended.

This is not to suggest that commodities do exchange at their values, the labour time socially necessary to produce them, including both direct (living) and indirect (dead) labour inputs – the labour time necessary to produce the produced means of production, i.e. raw materials, machinery, factory buildings, and so on. Market prices will be affected by the capital–labour ratios, scarcities, skills, monopolies, tastes and by more or less accidental variations in supply and demand. These contingent influences have been the primary object of study of orthodox economists since the neoclassical revolution of the 1870s, with little advance being made on Adam Smith's ideas of the 1770s, except through increasing mathematical sophistication. Marx did not ignore them, but they are irrelevant for uncovering the social relations of production specific to capitalism. If this cannot be done on the assumption that commodities exchange at their values, it certainly cannot be done in the more complicated cases when they do not. Throughout this book, unless otherwise stated, it will be assumed that commodities exchange at their values. This is not to be interpreted as a fully-fledged price theory but as an attempt to understand the nature of the price *system*.

Thus, capitalism, as generalised commodity production for profit, is characterised by the production of social use values and, therefore, the exchange of the products of concrete labours that exist, and contribute to value, as abstract social labour. Methodologically, this is not an analytical imposition of the notion of value, but simply a reflection of what the market system *does* – it connects concrete labours with one another and measures them against each other. Marx did not base his concept of value on a mental construct removed from the real world and requiring all sorts of arbitrary assumptions. Rather, his argument is based upon the fact that the reduction of all types of labour to a common standard is a product of the real world of capitalism itself. Marx's labour theory of value first and foremost reproduces in thought the way in which capitalism actually organises the production of the goods and services necessary for social reproduction. It recognises that the relationship between commodities as use values (relative prices) is the outcome of an underlying social relationship between the producers that expresses the equivalence between their different concrete labours as abstract social labour. The important point is that the relationship between exchange, prices and values is not exclusively, or even primarily, quantitative; it reflects definite social relations of production, distribution and exchange. It is these that must be understood.

Labour and Labour Power

The previous section has shown that, in capitalist society, the exchange of different types of labour products takes place through the exchange of commodities. This could occur without capitalism, for example if a society of independent artisans exchanged their products, often termed simple commodity production. However, this is more a logical possibility than ever a historically dominant mode of production. What characterises capitalism is not the exchange of the products of independent producers, but the purchase and sale of the workers' capacity to labour and its use in commodity production for profit.

To distinguish the workers from their ability or capacity to work, Marx called the latter *labour power*, and its performance or application *labour*. The most important distinguishing feature of capitalism is that labour power becomes a commodity. The capitalist is the purchaser, the worker is the seller, and the price of labour power is the wage. The worker sells labour power to the capitalist, who determines how that labour power should be exercised as labour to produce particular commodities. As a commodity, labour power has a use value, which is the creation of other use values. This property is independent of the particular society in which production takes place. However, in capitalist societies use values are produced for sale and, as such, embody abstract labour time or value. In these societies, the commodity labour power also has the specific use value that it is the source of value when exercised as labour. In this, labour power is unique.

The worker is not therefore a slave in the conventional sense of the word and sold like other commodities, but owns and sells labour power. Also, the length of time for which the sale is made or formally contracted is often very short. Yet in many other respects the worker is like a slave. There is little or no control over the labour process or product. There is the freedom to refuse to sell labour power, but this is a partial freedom, the alternative in the limit being starvation or social degradation. One could as well argue that a slave could flee or refuse to work although the level and immediacy of retribution are of a different order altogether. For these reasons the workers under capitalism have been described as wage slaves, although the term is an oxymoron. You cannot be both slave and wage worker – one does not have the freedoms that the other must enjoy.

On the other side to the class of workers are the capitalists who control the workers and the product of labour through their command of wage payments and ownership of the tools and raw materials or means of production. This is the key to the property relations specific to capitalism. For the capitalist monopoly of the means of production ties the workers to the wage relation, explained above. If the workers owned or were entitled to use the means of production independently of the wage contract, there would be no need to sell labour power rather than the product on the market and, therefore, no need to submit to capitalist control both during production and outside, in society.

Now we see that the labour theory of value not only captures the distributional relationships established through the exchange of labour products, but also embodies the more fundamental relations of production specific to capitalism, once the distinction between labour and labour power is drawn. The social exchange of labour power for money, in addition to the exchange of the products of labour through the market, presupposes the monopoly of the means of production by the class of capitalists, on the one hand, and the existence of a class of wage workers with no direct access to the means of production, on the other (see chapter 6). Not surprisingly, this critically important distinction between labour and labour power is never drawn in mainstream economics with its 'neutral' terminology of factor inputs and outputs. This terminology suggests that the labour and capital inputs contribute in the same way to the production process, so much so that workers are conceptualised as 'human capital', thereby reduced to the status of physical inputs (as is 'capital' itself, rather than being seen as the result of historically-specific class relations).

The Fetishism of Commodities

Marx perceives that the exchange of produced use values reflects the social organisation of labour that has produced these commodities. But to many of his contemporary economists and to nearly all subsequent ones, the relationship between workers and the products of their labour remains merely a relationship between things, that is to say, of the type x loaves of bread = 1 shirt, or one worker-week is worth so much of a standard of living (the wage bundle). Thus, while capitalism organises production in definite social relationships between capitalists and workers, these relationships are expressed and appear, in part, as relationships between things. These social relations are further mystified when money enters into consideration, and everything is analysed in terms of price. Marx calls such a perspective on the capitalist world the *fetishism of commodities*. It is most apparent in modern economics, where even labour power is treated as an input or factor like any other. Factor rewards are seen first and foremost as due to the physical properties of the inputs, as if profit or rent were directly produced by machinery or land, rather than by people existing together in particular relationships and societies.

Marx draws the brilliant parallel between commodity fetishism and feudal religious devotion. God is humanity's own creation. Under feudalism, human relationships with God conceal and justify the actual relationships to fellow beings, an absurd bond of exploitation as it appears to the bourgeois (capitalist) mind. Capitalism, however, has its own God and bible. The relationship of exchange between things is also created by people, concealing the true relationship of exploitation and justifying this by the doctrine of freedom of exchange.

But there is a major difference between religious and commodity fetishism. For, whereas God is a creation of religions, commodities do have a real existence, and their exchange represents and, to some extent, conceals the real social relationships of production (see chapter 1). Similarly, the price system does exist and is attached to the broader economic and social system, but without making the nature of that system transparent. In particular, buying and selling commodities does not reveal the circumstances by which they have come to the market, or the exploitation of the direct producers, the wage workers, by the capitalist class. Consequently, Marx's emphasis is upon prices as a value system, determined by the class relations of production and exploitation. But it is worth emphasising that it is not only class and production relations that are fetishised by their commodity form. Only by tracing back from the marketplace through to production can we pierce through the veil of advertising and discover whether products are, for example, environmentally friendly ('organic'), or free from exploitation of child labour, and so on.

In this light, commodity fetishism can be made the basis of a theory of alienation or reification. Not only are the workers divorced from the control of the product and the process of producing it, but also the view of this situation is normally distorted or at most partial. Further, the capitalists are subject to social control through competition and the need for profitability. For both capitalists and workers, it appears that external powers exert this control, and not the social relations of production and their effects peculiar to capitalism. Once again, there is a sense in which this is true. For example, the loss of employment or bankruptcy may be blamed on a thing or an impersonal force, as in the unfortunate breakdown of a machine, changes in consumer preferences, international competition or an economic crisis of whatever origin or cause. Most recently, 'globalisation' has been understood in generic, almost religious, terms as being able to explain all things good or bad about contemporary capitalism (see chapter 14). But to breathe analytical and explanatory life into competition, economic crisis and globalisation, and go beyond mysticism, we must start with a clear understanding of the social relations underpinning capitalist production, rather than fetishise its effects.

The distinction between religious and commodity fetishism is not simply academic. Because of its imaginary origins, religious fetishism can readily be rejected, at least in theory, although in reality it can be buttressed by material forces and practices giving it considerable power and influence over our daily lives. By contrast, however well it is understood, it is not possible to wish away the price system by an act of will, except in marginal instances and fragile attempts at self-sustainability. As a result, and here again there is a parallel with religious fetishism, underlying capitalist realities are grasped from time to time through the consequences of daily practices and reflection upon them, and thereby become the subject of both material and ideological struggle. The existence of profits, interest and rent indicates that capitalism is exploitative; and unemployment, economic crises, vast inequalities, environmental degradation, and so on, are no less transparent than the inability of the meek to inherit the world and to eat pie in the sky when they die.

This raises two closely related and hotly debated issues within Marxism and across the social sciences and the political spectrum more generally. The first is the methodological and analytical question of how to order the diverse empirical outcomes associated with capitalism. Can we deal with inequality independent of class, poverty apart from economic and other forms of repression, and growth separately from crisis? Second, to what extent are such conditions endemic to, or reformable within, capitalism? For it is not simply a matter of the logical connections between the different categories of political economy, between value and price for example. One of the strengths of Marx's *Capital*, acknowledged by friend and foe alike, is to have pointed to the systemic character of capitalism, and to its essential features. By the same token, Marxism's antipathy to reformism other than as part of a broader strategy for socialism is based on its inevitable limitations within the confines imposed by capitalism. Around these issues, there remains much room for dispute over method, theory and the politics of reform, both within and with Marxism.

Such perspectives shed light on Marx's own intellectual development. For his later concept of commodity fetishism forges a link with his earlier work of 1844. Then, while breaking with Hegelian idealism and adopting a materialist philosophy, he developed a theory of alienation. This concentrated on the individual's relationship to physical and mental activity, fellow beings and consciousness of these processes. In *Capital*, after extensive economic study, Marx is able to make explicit the coercive forces exerted by capitalist society on the individual. These can be the compulsion of profitability and wage labour, or the more subtle distortions by which these forces are ideologically justified: abstinence, the work ethic, freedom of exchange and other aspects of commodity fetishism. Unlike other theories of alienation, a Marxist theory places the individual in a class position and analyses the perceptions of that position. Each is not seen, in the first instance, as a powerless individual in an unexplained 'system' of irrationality, impersonality, inequality, authoritarianism, bureaucracy or whatever. These phenomena have their own character and function in capitalist society at a particular time. They can only be understood as a whole or in relation to individuals against the perspective of the workings of capitalism, as is explained in the following chapters.

Issues and Further Reading

Marx's value theory is extremely controversial among proponents and opponents alike. An essential starting point in assessing debates is the distinction between the approaches of Ricardo and Marx, with many erroneously identifying the two as holding to *the* (same) labour theory of value. But Ricardo simply counts labour time to explain price without investigating why products take the form of commodities. The latter is Marx's starting point, justifying value as a category in his approach since society itself, through the capitalist production process, the use of machinery and the market, undertakes the qualitative and quantitative comparison of (concrete) labour times. On this, see especially Geoffrey Pilling (1980), and the contributions in Ben Fine (1986) and Jesse Schwartz (1977, part 5).

Marx's theory of value is discussed extensively throughout his mature works, especially Marx (1976, part 1, and 1987). For a concise overview of the theory and its implications, see Marx (1981a, part 7, and 1998); see also Friedrich Engels (1998, part 2). The interpretation in this chapter draws upon Ben Fine (1980, ch. 6, 2001a, and 2002, ch. 3) and Alfredo Saad-Filho (2003b). For similar views, see Diane Elson (1979), Duncan Foley (1986, ch. 2), David Harvey (1999, ch. 1), Moishe Postone (1993) and John Weeks (1981, chs 1–2, and 1990). Duncan Foley (2000) and Alfredo Saad-Filho (1997a and 2002, ch. 2), and the contributions in Simon Mohun (1995), critically explain and review alternative interpretations of Marx's value theory.

3
Capital and Exploitation

In the previous chapter, it was shown that the production of use values as commodities, which is typical of capitalism, tends to conceal the social relations of production as a relationship between producers. It focuses attention, instead, on exchange as a relationship between things. Nevertheless, as simple commodity production demonstrates logically and a history of trade demonstrates in reality, exchange itself can and does exist without capitalism. It is only when labour power becomes a commodity, and wage workers are regularly hired to produce commodities for sale at a profit, that capitalism becomes the mode of production typical of a given society. In this chapter, by examining exchange from the perspective of the workers and then the capitalists, it will be seen why capitalism is not merely a system of commodity production but also, more crucially, a system of wage labour.

Exchange

Essential to exchange, beyond simple bartering (which is a very limited historical phenomenon), is money. The functions of money have been well explored in the literature. It is a measure of value, a standard of prices (i.e. a unit of account), a means of payment or exchange, and a store of value. As a means of payment it mediates the process of exchange, by settling transactions either simultaneously or in arrears (at any one time, this use may come into conflict with money's use as a store of value, and this is important in crises).

Consider initially a general problem: an individual owns some commodity but, for whatever reason, would prefer to exchange it for another. First, the commodity (*C*) must be exchanged for money (*M*). This sale is represented by *C* – *M*. Second, the money obtained is exchanged for the desired commodity, *M* – *C*. In both cases, *C* – *M* and *M* – *C*, commodity values are realised on the market; the seller obtains money and the buyer acquires a use value, which may be used either in consumption or production. In general, then, commodities are sold in order to purchase other commodities, and this can be represented by *C* – *M* – *C*, the circulation of commodities. The two extremes of commodity circulation are denoted by *C* because they are in commodity form and have the same value, not because they are the same thing – indeed they cannot be the same thing, otherwise the whole purpose of the exchange is defeated, speculative activity in commodities aside.

We presume that both commodities have the same value because commodity circulation (exchange) as such cannot add value to the goods or services being exchanged. Although some sellers can profit from the sale of commodities above value (unequal exchange), as with unscrupulous traders and speculators for example, this is not possible for every seller because whatever value one party gains in exchange must be lost to the other. In this light, simple commodity exchanges are summarised in figure 3.1.

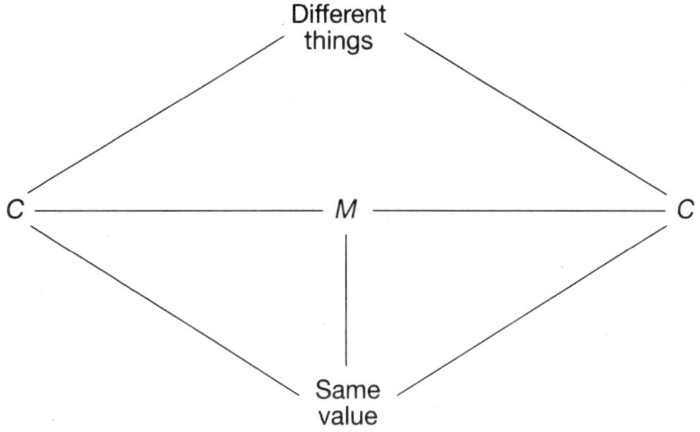

Figure 3.1 Simple commodity exchange: selling in order to buy

Typically, under capitalism, simple commodity exchanges can start with a worker or a capitalist. For the worker, the only commodity available to sell is her or his labour power, and this is exchanged for wages (*M*) and eventually for wage goods (*C*). Alternatively, the commodity sale *C* – *M* could also be undertaken by a capitalist, either in order to buy goods for personal consumption or to renew production, for example, through the subsequent purchase of labour power, raw materials, machines, and so on.

Capital

In contrast with simple exchanges, which start with commodity sales, capitalist production must start with the purchase of two types of commodities. These commodities are the means of production (inputs for further processing, machines, spare parts, fuel, electricity, and so on) and labour power. A necessary condition for the latter is the willingness on the part of the workers to sell this commodity. This willingness, an exercise of the 'freedom' of exchange, is forced on the workers, because they have no other way of satisfying their consumption needs. On the one hand, selling labour power is a condition of work, for otherwise the workers cannot gain access to the means of production, monopolised by capitalists. On the other hand, it is a requirement for consumption, as this is the only commodity that the workers are consistently able to sell (see chapters 2 and 6).

Having gathered together means of production and labour power ($M - C$), the capitalists organise and supervise the production process, and sell the resulting output ($C - M$). In the latter case, the dash conceals the intervention of production in the transformation of the commodity inputs into money (see chapter 4). For the moment, we can represent a capitalist's exchange activity by $M - C - M'$. In contrast to simple commodity exchange, $C - M - C$, discussed in the previous section, the capitalist circulation of commodities begins and ends with money, not commodities. This implies that at the two extremes one finds the same thing, money, rather than different things, commodities with distinct use values. Clearly, the only purpose in undertaking this exchange activity on a systematic basis is to get more value, rather than different use values (if less were the objective, money could be thrown away without any palaver). Since the motive of exchange is to expand value, M' must be numerically greater than M. The difference between *M′* and *M* is *s*, or *surplus value*. Capitalist exchanges are summarised in figure 3.2.

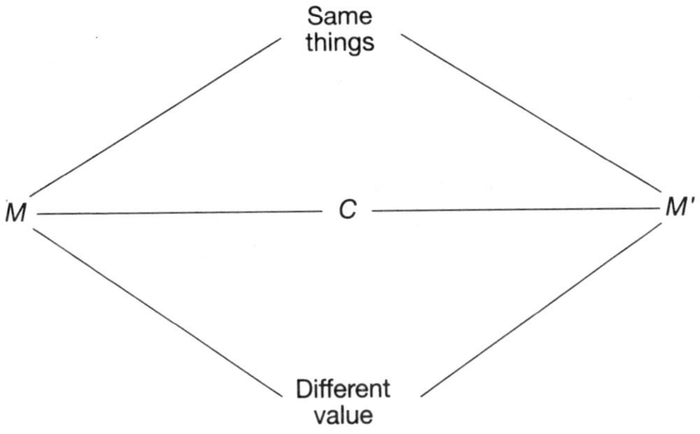

Figure 3.2 Capitalist exchange: buying in order to sell dearer (contrast with Figure 3.1)

Marx points out that capital is *self-expanding value*. Money acts as capital only when it is used to generate more money or, more precisely, when it is employed in the production of surplus value. This basic understanding of the nature of capital allows it to be distinguished from the various specific forms it assumes and the functions undertaken by those forms, whether it be as money, factor input or commodity. Each of these is capital only in so far as it contributes directly towards the expansion of the advanced value. As such it functions as capital, as well as performing its specific task as means of payment, depository of exchange value or means of production.

We have characterised capital through the activity of the industrial capitalists (which include not only manufacturing capital but also provision of services and other activities productive of surplus value). There are other forms of capital, though, namely merchant's capital and loan capital. Both of these also expand value by buying (merchandise or financial assets rather than means of production) in order to sell dearer. Both appear historically before industrial capital. It was Marx's insight to reverse their historical order of appearance, in order to analyse capitalism abstractly and in its pure form. This allows him to focus on the wage relation and the production of (surplus) value, without the complications introduced by forms and relations of exchange, including mercantilism or usury, which merely transfer value (for a more detailed analysis of these forms of capital, see chapters 11 and 12).

Surplus Value and Exploitation

Most economists might find this characterisation of capital as self-expanding value uncontroversial, even if a little odd. Looking back at figure 3.2, and with reference to figure 3.1, it is evident that although M and M' have different values, M and C have the same value. This implies that extra value has been created in the movement $C - M'$. This added (surplus) value is numerically equal to the difference between the values of outputs and inputs. The existence of surplus value (profit in its money form) is uncontroversial, for this is obviously the motive force of capitalist production, and $M - C - M'$ is clearly its general form. The problem is to provide an explanation for the *source* of surplus value.

This has already been located in production, above, by showing that exchange does not create value. Therefore, among the commodities purchased by the capitalist there must be one or more that creates more value than it costs. In other words, for surplus value production at least one commodity must contribute more labour time (value) to the outputs than it costs to produce as an input; therefore, its use value is the production of (surplus) value. As already indicated, this leaves just one candidate – labour power.

First, consider the other inputs. While they contribute value to the output as a result of the labour time socially necessary to produce them in the past, the quantity of value that they add to the output is no more nor less than their own value or cost – for otherwise money would be growing magically on trees or, at least, in machines. In other words, non-labour inputs cannot transfer more value to the output than they cost as inputs for, as was shown above, *equal* exchanges do not create value, and *unequal* exchanges cannot create surplus value.

Now consider labour power. Its value is represented by its cost or, more precisely, by the value obtained by the workers against the sale of their labour power. This typically corresponds to the labour time socially necessary to produce the real wage bundle, or the wage goods regularly purchased by the working class. In contrast, the value created by labour power in production is the labour time *exercised* in return for that wage. Unlike the other inputs, there is no reason why the contribution made by the workers to the value of the output (say, ten hours per day) should equal the cost of labour power (whose value may be produced in, say, five hours). Indeed, it can only be because the value of labour power is less than labour time contributed that surplus value is created.

Using labour time as the unit of account, it has been shown that capital can expand only if the value contributed by the workers exceeds the remuneration received for their labour power – surplus value is created by the excess of labour time over the value of labour power. Therefore, labour power not only creates use values: when exercised as labour it also creates value and surplus value. The strength of this argument is seen by its brief comparison with alternative theories of value.

Theories of abstinence, waiting or intertemporal preference depend upon the sacrifice by capitalists of present consumption as the source of profits. Nobody could deny that these 'sacrifices' (usually made in luxurious comfort) are a condition of profit, but like thousands of other conditions they are not a cause of profits. People without capital could abstain, wait and make intertemporal choices until they were blue in the face without creating profits for themselves. It is not abstinence that creates capital, but capital that requires abstinence. Waiting has existed in all societies; it is even to be found among squirrels. Similar conclusions apply to viewing risk as a source of profit. It must always be borne in mind that it is not things, abstract or otherwise, that create economic categories, for example profits or wages, but definite social relations between people.

Marginal productivity theories explain the increase in value between *C* and *M'* by the technically determined contributions of labour and capital goods to output. Such an approach can have no social content, no specific insight into the nature of labour and 'capital' when attached to *capitalism*. For labour and labour power (never clearly distinguished from one another) are treated on a par with *things*, while the theory has neither the interest in explaining, nor the capacity to explain, the social organisation of production. Only the quantities of means of production and labour power matter, as if production were primarily a technological rather than social process. However, factors of production have existed in all societies. The same cannot be said of profits, wages, rents or even prices, which are comparatively new historically speaking. Explanation of the form of the production process, the mode of social interaction and reproduction based upon it, and the categories to which they give rise, demands more than mainstream economic theory is able to offer.

Marx argues that all value (including surplus value or profit) is created by labour, and that surplus value is brought about by the exploitation of immediate, direct or living labour. Suppose that the average workday is ten hours, and that the wages correspond to half the value created in this labour time. Then for five hours each day work is 'free' for the capitalist class. In this case, the rate of exploitation, defined as the ratio of surplus to necessary labour time, is 5 hours divided by 5 hours, or 1 (100 per cent). Although Marx refers to the rate of surplus value when being specific about exploitation under capitalism, this concept could be similarly applied to other modes of production, for example feudalism with feudal dues or slavery. The difference is that, in these last two cases, the fact of exploitation is apparent while, under capitalism, exploitation in production is disguised by the freedom of exchange.

Denote surplus labour time by s and necessary labour time by v. Together s and v make up the living labour, l

(in money form, s is surplus value, v is called variable capital, and l is the newly produced value):

$$s + v = l$$

The rate of exploitation is $e = s/v$. Marx calls v variable capital because the amount of value that will be added by the workers, l, is not fixed in advance, when they are hired, but depends upon the amount of work that can be extracted on the production line, farm or office. It is variable in contrast to constant capital, c. This is not fixed capital (e.g. a factory, that lasts several production cycles) but, rather, the raw materials and the wear and tear on fixed capital, in so far as it is consumed during the period of production. For example, a machine that costs £100,000 and lasts ten years contributes £10,000 per annum to constant capital. The value of constant capital does not vary during production (only labour creates value), but is preserved in the output by the worker's labour, a service unwittingly performed for the capitalist. Clearly, c and v are both capital because they represent value in money form advanced by the capitalists in order to make profit. Therefore, the value λ of a commodity is made up of constant and variable capital plus surplus value (or, alternatively, constant capital plus living labour), $\lambda = c + v + s$. Its cost is $c + v$, leaving the surplus value (s) to form profit in money form.

Absolute and Relative Surplus Value

The surplus value produced depends on the rate of exploitation and the amount of labour employed (which can be increased by accumulation, see chapter 6). Assume that real wages remain unchanged. The rate of exploitation can be increased in two ways, and attempts to increase it will be made – for the nature of capital as self-expanding value imposes an important qualitative objective on the capitalists: profit maximisation, or at least that the growth of profitability should take a high priority.

First, e can be increased through what Marx calls the production of *absolute surplus value*. On the basis of existing methods of production – that is, the values of commodities remain the same – the simplest way to do this is through the extension of the working day. If, for the example given above, the working day is increased to eleven hours, with all else constant including the magnitude of wages, the rate of exploitation rises to 6/5 or 120 per cent. The production of absolute surplus value (s') is illustrated in figure 3.3 (total surplus value is $s + s'$).

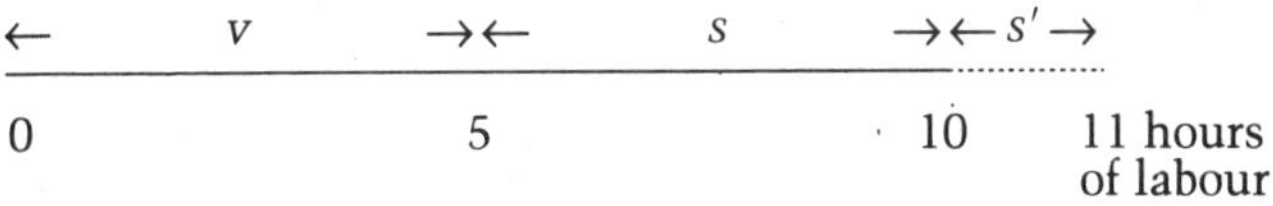

Figure 3.3 Production of absolute surplus value (s')

There are other ways of producing absolute surplus value. For example, if work becomes more intense during a given working day more labour would be performed in the same period, and absolute surplus value would be produced. The same result can be achieved through making work continuous without breaks either of limited duration or even for rest and refreshment. The production of absolute surplus value is often a by-product of technical change, because the introduction of new machines or conveyors in the production line also allows for the reorganisation of the labour process. This offers an excuse for the elimination of breaks or 'pores' in the workday, seen as sources of inefficiency for the capitalists, and leads to increased control over the labour process (as well as greater labour intensity), and higher profitability independent of the value changes brought about by the new machinery.

Alternatively, the desired pace of work within a given working day could be obtained through a crudely applied discipline. There may be constant supervision by middle management and penalties, even dismissal, and rewards. But more informal methods might also be employed. A system of wages based on piece-rates, for example, encourages the worker to set a high pace of work, while a premium for overtime is an inducement to work beyond normal hours (which must not absorb the entire extra surplus value, for otherwise there would be no additional profit involved for the capitalist).

Yet another way of producing absolute surplus value is the extension of work to the whole working-class family. It appears that children, wife and husband all receive a separate wage. But the structural role played by those wages is simply to provide the means to reproduce the working class family (and, therefore, the working class as a whole), rather than merely the individual labourers. With the extension of waged work to the whole family, it is possible through labour market pressure (lower wages due to more workers seeking employment) that more labour is provided for little or no increase in the value of wages as a whole.

However, there are limits in the extent to which capitalism can depend upon the production of absolute surplus value. Quite apart from the natural limits of 24 hours in the day, the physical and moral welfare and the resistance of the working class are barriers to the extraction of absolute surplus value. Nevertheless, absolute surplus value is always important in the early phases of capitalist development, when workloads tend to increase rapidly, and at any time it is a remedy for low profitability (even for developed capitalist countries) – if the medicine can be administered.

Relative surplus value does not suffer from the same limitations, and it tends to become the dominant method of increasing e as capitalism develops (see chapter 6). Relative surplus value is produced through the reduction of the value of labour power (v) by means of improvements in the production of the goods in the wage bundle (or, more generally, through the appropriation of productivity gains by the capitalist class). In this case, the working day remains the same, for example at ten hours, but, because of productivity gains, v falls from five to four hours, leaving a surplus value of six hours (e rises to 6/4 or 150 per cent). There are several ways to achieve this result, including increased co-operation and finer division of labour, use of better machinery, and scientific discovery and innovation. The production of relative surplus value is illustrated in figure 3.4. As a result of technical change, v falls to v', and relative surplus value is produced in addition to the old surplus value. This should be compared with figure 3.3.

The production of absolute surplus value can be based on the grim determination of individual capitalists using the threat of punishment, lock-outs and dismissal, although

Before technical change:

← v →← s →

0 5 10 hours of labour

After technical change (lower value of labour power):

← v' →← s' →

0 4 10 hours of labour

Figure 3.4 Production of relative surplus value

supportive state intervention is rarely found wanting when required. In contrast, production of relative surplus value depends critically upon all capitalists, since none alone produces a significant proportion of the commodities required for the reproduction of the working class. In particular, it depends upon competition and accumulation inducing the technical changes that bring down the value of labour power.

Machinery and Technical Change

Marx attaches great importance to the analysis of the way in which production develops under capitalism. He devotes considerable attention not only to the power relations between workers and capitalists, but also to the more specific question of the technical relations under which production takes place. In particular, for developed capitalism, he argues that the factory system necessarily predominates (rather than, for example, independent craft production or the putting-out system, in which capitalists provide inputs to handicraft workers, and later collect their produced commodities). Within the factory, the production of relative surplus value is pursued systematically through the introduction of new machinery.

New machinery increases productivity because it allows a greater amount of raw materials to be worked up into final products in a given labour time. Initially, the physical power of the worker will be replaced by the power of machinery. Later, the workers' tools will be incorporated into the machinery, so that ultimately the workers become minders or appendages of the machines – to feed the machines and watch over them, and to become their servants rather than vice versa (which may, nevertheless, require high levels of training and technical expertise).

The introduction of new machinery increases the intensity of work in a way that differs from that experienced under the production of absolute surplus value, for now machinery combines together what was previously a number of separate tasks. This has contradictory effects on the working class. They are deskilled by the machinery that displaces them and simplifies their tasks at work, but they are also required to command new skills as a number of simplified tasks is combined. Similarly, the physical burden of work is both lightened by the power of machinery but also increased through the higher pace and intensity of work.

To a large extent, this analysis presupposes a given set of products and production processes which are systematically transformed through the increasing use of machinery. Marx does not neglect, indeed he emphasises, the role of science and technology in bringing forth innovation in both products and processes. But quite clearly such developments cannot be the subject of a general theory of capitalist production since their extent and rhythm are contingent upon non-economic factors such as the progress of scientific discovery in different areas, the translation of discoveries into more productive technologies, and their successful introduction in the workplace. Nevertheless, Marx concludes that the factory system will lead to a massive increase in the ratio of physical capital to labour, what he termed the technical composition of capital (see chapter 8). On the one hand, this follows on by definition of productivity increase, as each labourer must work up more raw materials into final products (otherwise productivity would not have risen). On the other hand, this is a condition for productivity growth, since the mass of fixed capital in the form of machinery and factories must also increase.

Productive and Unproductive Labour

Marx's distinction between productive and unproductive labour is itself a corollary of his concept of surplus value. For Marx, labour is productive if it is hired in order to produce surplus value directly. This implies that productive labour is wage labour performed for (and under the control of) capital, in the sphere of production, and directly producing commodities for sale. The commodities produced and the type of labour performed are irrelevant.

All other types of wage labour are unproductive, for example, labour that is not hired by capital (e.g. the self-employed and most government employees), labour that is not directly employed in production (such as managers or workers employed in exchange activities, including the trade and financial sectors, as well as accountants, sales-people and cashiers even if they are employed by industrial capital), and workers not producing commodities for sale (e.g. housemaids and other independent providers of personal services).

The productive–unproductive distinction is specific to *capitalist* labour. It is determined by the social relations under which labour is performed, rather than the product of the activity, its usefulness or social importance. For example, doctors and nurses can perform either productive or unproductive labour, depending on their form of employment – at a private clinic or a public hospital, for example. Even though their activities are the same, and possibly equally valuable for society in some sense, in one case they provide a public service free at the point of delivery while, on the other, their employment is contingent upon the profitability of enterprise.

Although the unproductive workers do not directly produce surplus value, they are exploited if they work for longer than the value represented by their wage – being unproductive is no obstacle against capitalist exploitation! From the point of view of capital, unproductive sectors, for example retailing or banking, capture part of the surplus value produced in the economy (and, therefore, obtain the wherewithal to pay wages, other expenses and their own profits) through transfers from the value-producing sectors, via the pricing mechanism. For example, commercial capital purchases commodities below value and sells at value, whereas interest-bearing capital (including banks and other financial enterprises) obtains revenue primarily through the payment of customer fees and interest on loans (see chapters 11 and 12).

Issues and Further Reading

Volume 1 of *Capital* is in part concerned with the question: how is profit compatible with freedom of exchange? The answer given transforms the question into one of how surplus value is produced. This, in turn, is answered by reference to the unique properties of labour power as a commodity, and its capacity to produce both relative and absolute surplus value. Marx addresses these in the theoretical terms covered here but also in some empirical detail, focusing on changes in production methods themselves, especially the shift from manufacturing (literally production by hand) to the factory system. Marx's theory of capital and exploitation is explained in several of his works, especially Marx (1976, parts 2–6). The interpretation in this chapter draws upon Ben Fine (2001b, ch. 2) and Alfredo Saad-Filho (2002, chs 3–5, and 2003b). For similar approaches, see Chris Arthur (2001), Duncan Foley (1986, chs 3–4), David Harvey (1999, chs 1–2), Roman Rosdolsky (1977, part 3), John Weeks (1981, ch. 3) and the references cited in chapter 2.

Once the specificity of Marx's value theory and his emphasis on the uniqueness of labour power as a commodity are accepted, his theory of exploitation to explain surplus value and profit is relatively uncontroversial. It is necessary, though, to see surplus value as the result of coercion to work beyond the value of labour power rather than as a deduction from what the worker produces or as a share taken in the division of net product (as in what are termed Sraffian or neo-Ricardian approaches). On this, see Alfredo Medio (1977) and Bob Rowthorn (1980, especially ch. 1). Marx's theory of exploitation has inspired a rich vein of complementary analyses of the labour process both in its technical and in its organisational aspects. Science and technology are not simply improvement in technique but are governed, if not determined, by the imperative of profitability with the corresponding need to control and discipline labour (thereby influencing what is invented and how, and, similarly, what is adopted in production and how); see Brighton Labour Process Group (1977), Les Levidow (2003), Les Levidow and Bob Young (1981, 1985), Phil Slater (1980) and Judy Wajcman (2002). In addition, there is an imperative to guarantee sale (at a profit), with a corresponding departure in products and methods of sale from the social needs of consumers (however defined and determined) in pursuit of private profitability of producers, see Ben Fine (2002) for example.

Finally, the distinction between productive and unproductive labour is important as a starting point for examining the different roles played by industrial, financial, public sector and other workers in economic and social reproduction (see chapter 5). One debate has been over whether the distinction is valid or worthwhile – for example, on the grounds that all exploited (wage) labour should be lumped together as sources of surplus value. Another debate, between those who accept the distinction, concerns who should count as productive, ranging from a narrow definition of manual wage labour to a wider definition of all waged workers. Marx explains his categories of productive and unproductive labour in Marx (1976, appendix, and 1978a, ch. 4). These categories are discussed by Ben Fine and Laurence Harris (1979, ch. 3), Simon Mohun (2003), Isaak I. Rubin (1975, ch. 19 and 1979, ch. 24) and Sungur Savran and Ahmet Tonak (1999).

4
The Circuit of Industrial Capital

Volume 1 of *Capital* is largely self-contained, and it primarily gives a general analysis of capitalism and its process of development from the perspective of production – what are the social relations that allow capital to create surplus value and how do these give rise to economic and social developments around production? The other two volumes of *Capital* are devoted both to elaborating and to extending this general analysis. For this reason it is appropriate that the beginning of Volume 2 should analyse the circuit of capital. This is because it provides the basis for understanding a whole series of phenomena – commercial, interest-bearing and fixed capital, distribution of income and output, the turnover of capital, productive and unproductive labour, and crises – as well as providing an economic structure in which the social relations of production analysed in Volume 1 can be presented in more concrete form. In other words, Volumes 2 and 3 are about how the value relations of production, studied in Volume 1, give rise to more complex outcomes through the processes and structures of exchange and distribution.

The Money Circuit of Capital

Volume 2 begins with an account of the money circuit of capital. This is an expansion of the characterisation of capital as self-expanding value (see chapter 3), taking explicit account of the process of production. The general form of the circuit of industrial capital is:

$$M - C \ldots P \ldots C' - M'$$

Under the most general circumstances, and regardless of the commodity produced, the industrial capitalists advance money capital (M) in order to purchase commodity inputs (C), including labour power (LP) and means of production (MP). It should be realised that it is not money as money (money in its function as means of circulation or payment) that operates as capital in the above circuit. Quite the opposite. Money is necessary for the transactions but does not in itself make them possible. It is the separation in ownership of labour power from the means of production – a social and class relation of production – that allows a definite group of people (the capitalists) to hire others (the workers) in exchange for a wage. This can be stressed by explicitly separating the means of production and labour power in the circuit of capital:

$$M - C <^{MP}_{LP} \ldots P \ldots C' - M'$$

On purchase, the inputs (C) form productive capital (P). Production proceeds as labour power is exercised on the means of production, and the result is different commodity outputs (C'). C and C' are linked to P by dots to indicate that production has intervened between the purchase of inputs (C) and sale of outputs (C'). The commodities produced are denoted by C' not because their use value is different from that of the means of production (although this is generally the case), but because they contain surplus value over and above the value of the advanced capital, *M*. This is shown by the sale of the output for more money capital, $M' > M$.

It was shown in chapter 3 that surplus value, $s = \Delta M$, where Δ means difference or change, is created in production by the purchase of labour power at a value below the labour time expended (value created) in production. Surplus value makes its first appearance in commodity form immediately after production. Since the inputs (especially labour power, tools and machines) seem symmetrical in their contribution to output, it is easy to credit the creation of surplus value to the productivity of *all* the factor inputs without distinction. In contrast, it is difficult to credit surplus value to the excess of actual over necessary labour time, because the appearance of surplus value is delayed until after production has taken place, whereas the free exchange of labour power for its value takes place before production (even if the wages are paid in arrears).

The produced value (and surplus value) is now converted into money, by the sale of the output on the market. Having obtained sales income *M'*, the capitalists can renew the circuit of capital, either on the same scale (by renewing the original advance, *M*, with given prices and technologies, and spending the surplus value on consumption), or embark on an expanded productive circuit, through the investment of part of the surplus value (see below, and chapter 5).

The Circuit as a Whole

It was shown above (and in chapter 3) that capital is the social relation involved in the self-expansion of value: the production, appropriation and accumulation of surplus value. Capital, being self-expanding value, is essentially a process, the process of reproducing value and producing new value. In other words, capital is value in the process of reproducing itself as capital. The circuit of capital describes this motion, and it highlights the fact that capital takes different forms in its circuit or reproduction process. The social relation that is capital successively assumes and relinquishes as clothing the forms of money, productive capital and commodities.

The circuit of industrial capital is best represented by a circular flow diagram (see figure 4.1). This circuit is important for laying out the basic structure of the capitalist economy, and how the spheres of production and exchange are integrated with one another through the movement of capital as (surplus) value is produced, distributed and exchanged. As the circuit repeats itself, surplus value (s) is thrown off. This shows that capital as self-expanding value embraces not only definite social relations of production, but is also a circular movement going through its various stages. If s is accumulated for use as capital, we can think of expanded reproduction as being represented by an outward spiral movement.

Industrial capital changes successively into its three forms: money capital (M), productive capital (P) and commodity capital (C'). Each form presupposes the existence of the other two because it presupposes the circuit itself. This allows us to distinguish the specific function of each of the forms of capital from its general function as capital. In societies where they exist, money, factor inputs and commodities can always function, respectively, as means of payment, means of production or a

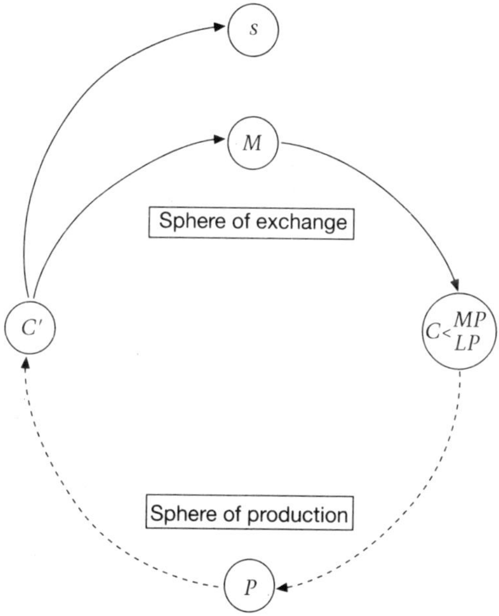

Figure 4.1 The circuit of capital

depository of exchange value, but they only serve as *capital* when they follow these functions sequentially in the circuit of capital. Then, money capital acts as a means of purchasing labour power, productive capital acts as a means of producing surplus value, and commodity capital acts as the depository of surplus value to be realised as money on sale.

In the movement through the circuit, two spheres of activity can be identified: production and circulation (exchange). The sphere of production lies between *C* and

C'. In this sphere, use values are transformed and value and surplus value are created. This has profound implications for Marx's theory of distribution, because it explains what there is to be distributed as well as the structures and processes of distribution of goods and values in the economy. The sphere of circulation contains the process of exchange between C' and C, and the realisation of surplus value, s.

It was shown in chapter 3 that even if capital and labour are used in the exchange process they add no value to the output. This conclusion seems strange to mainstream economists because they are usually interested in obtaining a price theory by aggregating the (supposedly independent) contribution of all the factors used in production *and* exchange. But Marx is interested in the social relations of production and distribution, and in the method of distributing the values newly produced during the circuit. For example, he argues that whereas commercial capital adds no value, this does not prevent its receiving a share of the value produced (see chapter 11).

By constructing the circuit of capital in circular form, as in figure 4.1 above, it becomes arbitrary to open and close the circuit with money capital, just as a circle has neither beginning nor end. Note that the money circuit contains the interruption of the sphere of circulation by the sphere of production. In characterising capital as self-expanding value, it has been shown that the capitalists' motive is to buy in order to sell dearer. So, for capital seen from the perspective of the money circuit, production appears as a necessary but unfortunate (and even wasteful) interruption in the process of money-making. Merchant's and interest-bearing capital avoid this interruption, although they depend upon production elsewhere. However, what is true for an individual capital does not hold for all (or even most) capitals. If a nation's capitalists are seized by the attempt to make profit without the unavoidable link of production, they will find themselves in a speculative boom which eventually crashes when the economy is brought back to the reality of the need for production – the only possible source of the value required to pay dividends, settle debts, service interest commitments and clear financial obligations (see chapters 7 and 12).

Marx also analyses the circuit from two other perspectives, from productive capital and from commodity capital. The circuit of productive capital begins and ends with *P*, production. The purpose of the circuit appears to be production and, in so far as surplus value is accumulated, production on an extended scale. In contrast to the money circuit, for the productive circuit the sphere of circulation appears as a necessary but unwanted intervention in the process of production. But it has already been shown, above, that it is not sufficient to produce (surplus) value; it has to be realised on sale. Economists more often than capitalists tend to ignore this necessary but uncertain mediation by exchange, for a capitalist who unwittingly or otherwise produces a growing inventory of commodities with the expectation or hope of future sale is soon brought back to reality with the loss of working capital. Finally, the circuit of commodity capital begins and ends with *C′*, and so its purpose appears to be to generate consumption. As the sphere of circulation is followed by the sphere of production, neither sphere is interrupted by the other, so neither appears as unnecessary or wasteful.

The three circuits of capital are formed out of the circuit as a whole. One might wonder why there are not four circuits of capital, with each 'node' on the circuit (*P*, *C′*, *M* and *C*) forming a starting and finishing point. The reason why *C* is not the basis for a circuit of capital is that it is not capital. The purchased means of production may be another capitalist's commodity production and hence commodity capital. However, labour power is never capital until it is purchased, and then it becomes productive capital and not commodity capital, which must contain produced surplus value. Thus, while from a technical point of view capitalism can be self-reliant for raw materials, it always and necessarily depends on the social reproduction of labour power from outside the pure system of production (see chapter 5). This entails the use of political, ideological and legal as well as economic power. The point is to get the labourer to work. The same problems do not exist in getting a machine to work.

It has been shown above that different views of capital's process of reproduction can be constructed, corresponding to each circuit of capital. These need not be uncritical of capitalism, but individually they are always inadequate, stressing one or more of the processes of production, consumption, exchange, profit-making and accumulation at the expense of the others. For example, only fleetingly, as they enter the circuit, do labour power and produced means of production appear separated and then, not forming capital, they do not generate a view of the circuit as a whole. Partly for this reason, mainstream economic theory can eliminate class relations altogether. However, these relations do enter mainstream theory as distributional or exchange relations, and not those of production.

In contrast, the money circuit suggests models of exchange. For mainstream economics, the matching of supply and demand becomes the be all and end all, and capital and labour are merely seen as productive services. Difficulties are merely associated with the informational services performed by the price (and interest rate) mechanism. The productive circuit, in turn, tends to ignore the market, and neoclassical and most growth theories can be cited in this context. This yields an excellent input–output analysis of economic reproduction, but the economy is not clearly capitalist at all. Finally, the commodity circuit is reflected in neoclassical general equilibrium theory, where supply and demand harmoniously interact through production and exchange to yield final consumption. It leads to the popular myth that the purpose of production is consumption (rather than profit or exchange). It is well-illustrated by Edgeworth box diagrams familiar to economics students. One of the strengths of Marx's circuit of capital is to expose the limitations of these outlooks. At the same time, it reveals the functions of the forms in which capital appears and constructs a basis on which major economic categories and phenomena can be understood.

Issues and Further Reading

Marx's analysis of exchange, especially in Volume 2 of *Capital*, has been relatively neglected despite the insights it offers. Often an approach has been adopted of complementing his theory of production with Keynesian theory of effective demand as if the two aspects of Marx's theory were subject to separate treatments. As suggested here and in Marx's own account, production and exchange are structurally separated but integrally related through the circuits of capital. Karl Marx's own analysis of the circuit of capital is developed in Karl Marx (1976, part 2 and 1978b, parts 1–2). It is explained in Ben Fine (1980, ch. 2) and Alfredo Saad-Filho (2002, chs 3–5). On Volume 2 of *Capital,* see Chris Arthur and Geert Reuten (1998). For similar interpretations as those offered here, see David Harvey (1999, ch. 3) and Roman Rosdolsky (1977, part 4). The concepts of money as money and money as capital are explained by Costas Lapavitsas (2003a) and Roman Rosdolsky (1977, part 3).

5
Economic Reproduction

The previous chapter examined a single circuit of industrial capital. For capital as a whole, there are a large number of different circuits, each moving at its own pace and each expanding at its own rate, and these circuits must be integrated with each other. Marx analyses these processes in Volume 2 of *Capital* by dividing the economy into two broad sectors, department 1, which produces means of production (*MP*, purchased with constant capital, *c*) and department 2, which produces means of consumption (purchased by workers out of variable capital, *v*, and by capitalists out of surplus value, *s*). This chapter examines the process of reproduction of capital as a whole. It begins with *simple reproduction*, where there is no capital accumulation. It subsequently examines *expanded reproduction*, where part of the surplus value is invested. Finally, it considers the social reproduction of the capitalist economy.

Simple Reproduction

In figure 5.1, the balance between departments 1 and 2 in conditions of simple reproduction is illustrated by a flow diagram. The two circuits are shown, $M_1 - C_1 \ldots P_1 \ldots C'_1 - M'_1$, and $M_2 - C_2 \ldots P_2 \ldots C'_2 - M'_2$ (with M'_1 and M'_2

being absorbed into the central pool of money, M). The figure also shows the commodity flows, with workers and capitalists buying consumption goods from department 2 with their wages, v_1 and v_2, and surplus value, s_1 and s_2, and capitalists buying means of production, c_1 and c_2, from department 1 (workers do not buy means of production, and we ignore savings).

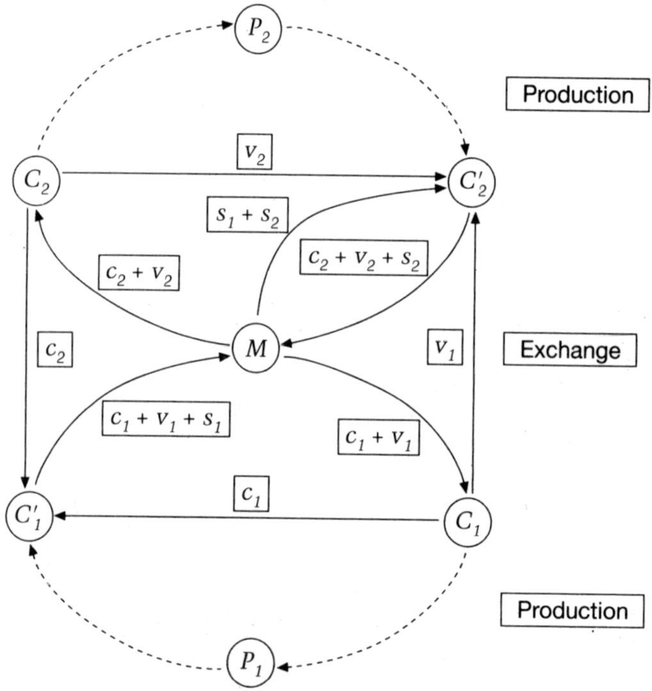

Figure 5.1 Economic reproduction

If there is no technical change, and if the capitalists spend all their surplus value on consumption and merely repeat the previous pattern of production, the economy can reproduce itself at the same level of activity, what Marx calls simple reproduction. This implies a certain balance between the values produced by the two departments. The value of output of department 1 is $c_1 + v_1 + s_1$, and the value of its sales of means of production is $c_1 + c_2$. So:

$$c_1 + v_1 + s_1 = c_1 + c_2$$

For department 2, similarly, the equality of values of output and value of sales of means of consumption gives:

$$c_2 + v_2 + s_2 = v_1 + v_2 + s_1 + s_2$$

Both the above expressions simplify to:

$$v_1 + s_1 = c_2$$

This is Marx's famous equation for balance between the two departments in simple reproduction.

Expanded Reproduction

If, however, capitalists do not consume their entire surplus value, but spend part of it buying additional means of production, capital accumulation takes place. In this case, capitalists' purchases of means of production, $c_1 + v_1 + s_1$, for the next period exceed current use, $c_1 + c_2$. It follows that, for expanded reproduction, $c_1 + v_1 + s_1 > c_1 + c_2$:

$$v_1 + s_1 > c_2$$

with the extent of the inequality depending upon the rate of accumulation.

These reproduction schema have been interpreted in a number of different ways. One of the most popular is that they offer a Marxian analysis of *equilibrium*, either static (in the case of simple reproduction) or dynamic (expanded reproduction). Alternatively, taking mainstream equilibrium growth theory as its model (often unwittingly), expanded reproduction is simply seen as an enlarged version of simple reproduction. The economy looks the same in all respects except that it is bigger.

Neither interpretation is within the spirit of Marx's own intentions. First, his methodology is sharply opposed to the use of equilibrium as an organising concept for the analysis of capitalism. Second, in the reproduction schema Marx is concerned to show how, despite the chaotic co-ordination of different producers through the sphere of exchange, in the absence of a conscious plan, *both* simple *and* expanded reproduction exist within the capitalist system. Therefore, simple and expanded reproduction are not alternatives, either theoretically or empirically. Rather, the former exists within the latter: expanded reproduction simultaneously depends upon and breaks with the conditions associated with simple reproduction that are its starting point – both in aggregate value magnitudes, and in the values of commodities themselves as these are subject to productivity increase as a result of accumulation. Furthermore, Marx never draws the implication, as in general equilibrium theory or for the proponents of *laissez-faire*, that different producers and consumers are harmoniously co-ordinated through the market at high levels of employment of resources. Rather Marx's schema points to two separate balances required by the reproduction and accumulation of capital.

The first is in values, as has already been illustrated above. The second is in use values, for the appropriate quantities of commodities have to be produced and exchanged with each other, both within and between the two departments. According to the schema above, the value quantities displayed have an unspecified quantitative relationship to the use values involved. This is clearly demonstrated by the hypothetical exercise of doubling the productivity (in other words, halving the values) of the commodities in one department while leaving those in the other unchanged. As a result, the value balance will be disrupted, even if the use value balance remains the same. This simple exercise shows that the two balances are to a degree independent of each other. However, they are not entirely independent of each other. Productivity change, for example, would eventually lead to the transfer of resources between the two departments. This involves the co-ordination across the economy between the two balances already specified, together with the complementary flows of money whose magnitudes are determined by the price system.

Meanwhile, the diagram of economic reproduction in figure 5.1 can be used to reinforce the (false or partial) views of the economy that were presented in the light of the single circuit of capital in the previous chapter. Little is added qualitatively, but the figure suggests what might be considered to be the factors determining the level of economic activity. Note, first, that mainstream economic theory and ideology tend to focus on the central 'box' of exchange activity, relative to which the two spheres of production appear to be extraneous. Generally, this supports the erroneous view that production can be taken for granted or that it is simply a technical relation that forms the unproblematic basis for exchange relations, as in the neoclassical production function.

This is most apparent for neoclassical general equilibrium theory (or *laissez-faire* economics) where exchange relations are considered sufficient to guarantee equality of supply and demand at full employment of economic resources. And, in stability analysis, it becomes a question of whether disproportion between the various quantities embodied within the circuits is self-correcting through price movements in response to excess supplies and demands.

For Keynesian theory, the role of aggregate demand becomes determinant. If we focus on the investment multiplier, the level of $c_1 + c_2$ assumes a central role. If we also include the role of consumption, then the expenditure on this out of national income, $v_1 + v_2 + s_1 + s_2$, also becomes important. In this form, the consumption function has more affinity with the post-Keynesian and Kaleckian methods of determining aggregate demand (where income is divided down into wages and profits). But the important point remains that, from these perspectives, a particular set of expenditure flows within the economy exercises a decisive influence on the level of aggregate economic activity. However, there is, in Marx's terms, no role for the production of surplus value and the conflict over this fundamental economic relation.

A more sophisticated post-Keynesian economics includes the role of money. In this respect, the level of economic activity is determined by the size of the flows of money streaming out of the central pool, *M*. Restrict these, either through entrepreneurial timidity or through contractionary monetary policies imposed by the central bank, and the economy falters. The respective roles of the banking system and the rate of interest are taken up in chapter 12. Here it is important to note that, from this point of view, the source of unemployment is to be found in insufficient exchange activity, almost irrespective of the ability of the economy to generate profitability. In Keynes's own theory, this depends largely on waves of pessimism, in which poor expectations about business profitability (and high expectations about interest rates) prove self-fulfilling prophecies. More generally, and in significantly different ways, recent developments within mainstream economic theory have given (so-called 'rational') expectations a considerably enhanced role in determining the path of the economy.

Finally, a more radical theory of the economy views the level of economic activity as being determined by distributional relations between capital and labour. Such a view is associated ideologically with both the right and the left, with the former arguing that the power of trade unions needs to be curbed to restore profitability, and the latter arguing that the conflicts involved are irreconcilable within the confines of capitalism. Analytically, this outlook depends on a 'fixed cake' understanding of the economy in which national income $v_1 + v_2 + s_1 + s_2$ is divided between the two classes with one gaining only at the expense of the other. For example, if wages, represented by $v_1 + v_2$, rise too much then profits, represented by $s_1 + s_2$, must fall, and this undermines both the motive and the ability to accumulate.

In spite of the appearances to the contrary, this view diverges sharply from Marx's own presentation of the structure of the capitalist economy. The attribution of a central role to distribution in the determination of profitability is only possible by confining the analysis to (one part of) the arena of exchange. Once the sphere of production is incorporated as well, the apparent symmetry between capital and labour, in distributional relations and in receiving profits and wages out of national income, evaporates, for the payment of wages is a *precondition* for the production process to begin (or, more exactly, this is true of the purchase of labour power, whose actual payment may well come later). In contrast, profits are the residual left after the payment of wages and other production costs, rather than being a 'piece of the cake' that may be negotiated in advance. For Marx, the distributional relations between capital and labour are not of the fixed cake variety, even if *ceteris paribus* profits are higher if wages are lower (although post-Keynesians might argue otherwise in view of inadequate demand). Profits depend first and foremost on the ability of capitalists to extract surplus value from the production process: whatever the level of wages, the capitalists need to coerce labour to work over and beyond the labour time required to produce those wages.

Uncertainty about the production of surplus value is only one of the aspects of uncertainty facing the capitalists. Four other types of uncertainty are also relevant. First, having produced surplus value, capitalists are uncertain about how much can be realised, until the output is finally sold. Second, the extraction of surplus value under competitive conditions leads to continuous productivity-enhancing technical change under capitalism. However, it was shown above that technical change disrupts the value and use value balances in the economy (and may contribute to antagonistic relations on the shopfloor), further increasing uncertainty. Third, as is shown in chapter 12, credit makes the resources of the financial system available to individual capitalists, facilitating the overexpansion of accumulation and creating conditions of financial and economic crisis. For example, credit could mislead industrial capitalists into anticipating favourable returns when none is forthcoming and, when fresh credit is used to pay for maturing obligations, the overexpansion of accumulation could create conditions of economic crisis. Finally, uncertainty becomes even greater when trading in money itself takes place, creating a class of money dealers only loosely connected to production and trade. Trading in money and money-related instruments is likely to lead to destabilising speculation and fraud, creating further uncertainty even for those not directly involved in such activities.

Thus it might be concluded, on the one hand, that for Marx the production of absolute and relative surplus value is crucial to the understanding of distributional relations, but that the latter cannot be read off from production conditions alone. On the other hand, uncertainty generated by the capitalist conditions of production (rather than deriving mainly from the shifting humours of the industrial and financial capitalists) plays an essential role in the production of surplus value as well as in the generation of crisis. They are inseparable from one another.

Social Reproduction

The previous sections have focused on simple and expanded reproduction from within the economic system alone. In fact, with one crucial exception the circuits of capital appear to be self-sustaining. The striking exception is labour power, for it is only reproduced within the circuits in so far as the provision of wage goods is adequate for that purpose. But, by virtue of the workers' freedom once the working day is over (as well as their resistance on the shopfloor and outside), capital must eventually release control over the process of reproduction and, in a sense, this is where social reproduction takes over. This process involves a complex array of non-economic relations, processes, structures, powers and conflicts. Interpreted in narrow terms, social reproduction includes the processes necessary for the reproduction of the workforce, both biologically and as compliant wage workers. More generally, social reproduction is concerned with how society as a whole is reproduced and transformed over time.

In short, and largely appropriately, social reproduction has become a catch-all phrase or umbrella within which to gather all non-economic factors. It covers the entire ground between the abstract category of *capital* and the empirical reality of *capitalism*. But this is only a partial understanding of the scope and significance of social reproduction. Capitalism clearly depends upon satisfactory economic as well as social reproduction, of which economic reproduction is a part, rather than being separate and independent. Misperception of the relationship between the two is commonplace, as if economic and social reproduction were separate from one another, like work and home. To a large extent, the inappropriate juxtaposition of the economic and the social (the latter as politics, culture or whatever), is most marked in the disciplinary boundaries between the social sciences.

One of the most significant sites of social and, increasingly, economic reproduction is the state. Through the state are constituted and expressed political relations, structures and conflicts that are distinct from, but not independent of, those of economic reproduction. The extent to which the state is dependent upon the economy is highly controversial, varying, if putting it in inappropriate one-dimensional terms, from those who argue the state is reducible to economic, especially capitalist, imperatives, to those who view the state as autonomous from the economy. The nature of the capitalist state will be taken up in chapter 14, but the issues here of what has been termed reductionism, on the one hand, and autonomy, on the other, are of more general methodological, theoretical and empirical significance. The important point is to recognise both the causal significance of the capitalist economy for the non-economic – what sort of state, property law, customs, politics, and so on prevail – and that these are themselves formed with effects that are conditioned but not determined by the economic.

Of course, similar considerations apply to those areas of social reproduction that lie outside the immediate orbit of the state, what is often referred to as 'civil society'. Social reproduction also depends upon the household or family system and the more general areas of private activity, not least consumption and other activities of the working class that induce and enable it to present itself for work on a daily basis. The emphasis so far has been upon the social reproduction of labour, but economic reproduction is equally dependent upon the formation and transformation of the conditions that enable the circuits of capital as a whole to be reproduced – not least the market, monetary and credit systems which require laws, regulations, and so on. These promote the interests of some capitalists at the expense of others, as well as preventing rivalry between capitalists from being unduly destructive. Such matters are equally the subject of politics, the state and civil society. At an abstract level, only the conditions necessary for, and induced by, economic reproduction can be identified alongside the way in which economic and social reproduction are structured in relation to one another. How is the accumulation of capital accommodated socially and conflict over it conducted and, generally, directed and contained? To progress further than this, it is necessary to introduce some degree of historical specificity, a task beyond the scope of this text.

Issues and Further Reading

As suggested in the previous chapter, Marx's analysis in Volume 2 of *Capital* has been neglected and so has been relatively free of controversy. The same cannot be said of social reproduction. It has been heavily debated whether with or within Marxism or not. Controversy covers the relationship between the economic and the non-economic (and how they do or do not depend upon one another), and the different aspects of the non-economic itself, from the nature of the autonomy of the state and politics to the role of 'civil society'.

This chapter focuses on the material contained in Karl Marx (1978b, part 3). The interpretation of social reproduction developed above draws upon Ben Fine (1992b), Ben Fine and Ellen Leopold (1993) and Ben Fine, Michael Heasman and Judith Wright (1996); see also John Weeks (1983). The value of labour power and the reproduction of the working class are discussed by Ben Fine (1998, 2002, 2003) and Alfredo Saad-Filho (2002, ch. 4); see also Kenneth Lapides (1998) and Michael Lebowitz (2003a).

6
Accumulation of Capital

The previous chapters have characterised capitalism as a mode of production. This provides a framework in which capital accumulation, and the historical development of capitalism as the world's dominant mode of production, can be understood. For, having uncovered the relations of production specific to capitalism, the systemic forces behind their creation and development can be isolated from the mass of phenomena taking place more or less simultaneously.

Marx devotes large sections of Volume 1 of *Capital* to the task of interpreting the genesis of British capitalism and the fundamental role played by the compulsion to accumulate. This must stand as a major application and confirmation of his conception of historical change. Here only an outline of his work can be offered. For more depth, those interested should consult *Capital* itself for Marx's own analysis, and later Marxists for more concrete studies of the causes, nature, timing and location of the first and subsequent capitalist transitions and 'industrial revolutions'.

Primitive Accumulation

An essential feature of capitalism is the existence of labour power as a commodity. A necessary condition for this is the separation of labour from ownership or claim to the means of production. The workers depend upon somebody else to provide these, for if the workers had unmediated access to the means of production, the product of labour rather than the capacity to work would be sold (if market exchange of products could persist in such circumstances). On the other side of the coin must be the capitalist with money to advance to purchase labour power and the wherewithal to maintain ownership of the means of production. The historical establishment of these social relations of production out of the feudal ones holds the key to the birth of capitalism.

In any society beyond the most primitive there will be saving of produce to form means of production for the future, whether it be in the form of hunting weapons, corn seed, animal stock or other implements. One of the distinguishing features of capitalism is the increase in the rate of savings. Marx found it commonplace, once capitalism had been established, for economists to attribute its creation to the self-sacrifice of energetic entrepreneurs, ploughing back their meagre profits into their businesses. More recently, the fact that, in poor countries, too small a part of the national income is saved is considered by many development economists as a major barrier to development.

Marx pours scorn on such a limited outlook. Capitalism is founded upon the forcible separation of the workers from the existing means of production. In Britain, this separation was imposed by large landowners, the aristocracy and the state, rather than being the cumulative outcome of individual thrift and selfless devotion to work in small farms and family enterprises. It entailed the conversion of the traditional (feudal) use of existing means of production and labour power into their social use in capitalistic organisation. This does not require, in the first instance, any additional accumulation of means of production or even their more efficient use, just their redistribution and operation according to new relations. Once this has occurred the process of competitive accumulation gathers its own momentum (see below, and chapters 3 and 4).

Since agriculture was, by far, the dominant sector of production in the pre-capitalist era, both in terms of output and volume of employment, this sector contained the source of a class of 'free' wage labourers. The secret of primitive or early accumulation of capital lay, then, in the expropriation of the agricultural population from the land, and the destruction of the right or custom of individual independent cultivation (even if feudal dues needed to be paid). This could be undertaken on an individual basis by landowners responding to the growing imperative of market exchanges. For example, it might arise out of pressures due to the accumulation of debt by the landowners, the impact of secular inflation, higher prices of wool relative to grain requiring less labour in the fields, and so on. Whatever their immediate causes, these transformations required the power of the state to make any headway in a violent and violently resisted process. State intervention, representing the interests of the emerging capitalist class, was twofold. First, enclosure movements dispossessed the peasantry of both common and individual land usage; resistance was fierce, generalised and brutally crushed. The class of landless labourers was created. Second, wage legislation and perverse systems of 'social security', culminating in the infamous Poor Law of 1834, forced long hours and industrial discipline on the landless labourers. The combined impact of these transformations was to turn the majority of the peasants into wage workers, creating the potential source of absolute surplus value.

Here Marx's emphasis is on the conversion of the method of use of the existing means of production, rather than their accumulation. No doubt technical progress and the reorganisation of production contributed to the rise in agricultural output that was to feed industry as well as the industrial proletariat. Simultaneously, but secondarily, technical progress also contributed to the rise in manufacturing output demanded as inputs for agricultural production. However, few labourers felt the gain of this increased output and, for those who did, it must have paled into insignificance against the deterioration of working conditions and the destruction of a way of life. Illustrative of this is the essential role played by physical force and the state in the creation of the proletariat, including the police, the army, the tax and justice systems, and so on, rather than the smooth operation of market forces. This contrasts with most present-day labour relations, where the dull compulsion of economic needs and their development through tradition, education and habit induces the working class to look upon the conditions of the capitalist mode of production as self-evident and morally justified. Force rarely needs to be at the forefront now (although it is available if required) because labour is deeply tied to capital and appears as if it always has been and always will be.

This extremely brief account explains the origins of the capitalist relations of production. By the seventeenth century the first enclosure movement (another was to follow in the eighteenth century) had been completed, creating a landless labouring class as well as a class of capitalists that first appeared as farmers. In the eighteenth century the use of the national debt, the taxation system, trade protection and the exploitation of colonies to accumulate wealth had reached its climax. The combination of labour and wealth in capitalist relations accompanied these processes, with the nineteenth century heralding the rapid pace of technological innovation and the accelerated growth of industrial society.

It is as well to recognise, however, that the creation of capitalism in Britain has been rather different from elsewhere. The forcible dispossession of the peasantry from the land was more extensive than in the rest of Europe, and its character was quite different from similar developments in other parts of the world. In Britain, a larger proportion of the population was transformed into wage workers. This was done through the creation of a system of large-scale landed property, so that a relatively small number of aristocrats came to hold the vast majority of privately owned land. Elsewhere in Europe, as well as in the north-eastern United States, the peasantry, or sections of it, proved better able to defend itself by taking possession of the land in smaller parcels, thereby making themselves independent of wage labour to a much greater extent.

The significance of these differences persists to the present day, with Britain's agriculture continuing to be characterised by larger farms and Britain's working population containing many fewer employees (and self-employed) in the agricultural sector than the rest of Europe. However, while Marx's analysis of primitive accumulation focuses on Britain, and to that extent deals with something of an exception, his analysis of the formation of the class of wage labourers out of the agricultural population remains an essential starting point for the study of capitalist transitions in other parts of the world.

While, for Marx, the crucial element in the transition to capitalism is the formation of a class of wage workers out of pre-capitalist class relations, this leaves open the immediate causes and mechanisms by which such transitions are achieved. These are diverse and complex, ranging over the different factors in the formation of markets both before and after the transition, from the role of the state to the access to credit, export markets, and so on. Not surprisingly, then, as already observed, transitions to capitalism have not only been varied in content and trajectory but they have also been heavily debated both within Marxism and between Marxism and other approaches.

The Development of Capitalist Production

In Britain capitalism came to the fore gradually, largely through the coincidence of favourable economic conditions – the discovery and hoarding of precious metals and low rents and wages, as well as proactive economic policies, inspired in part by mercantilism. The subsequent genesis of industrial capitalism was less protracted, developing more out of artisans and guilds and depending upon the absorption of the workers pushed out by capitalistic farming. A domestic market was simultaneously created for the produce of industrial capital by the ending of the peasantry's largely self-sufficient livelihood. Previously they had been generally able to serve their own needs through their control of the means of production (especially land and agricultural tools) according to feudal custom. With the advent of capitalism, the remaining independent producers needed money to advance to purchase the seeds, tools and other agricultural implements – which contributed to their transformation into wage workers. Thus capital does not necessarily destroy household production because of its superior efficiency. Indeed, household production persists even today, for example, in sweatshops. Rather, independent production is destroyed (or, more generally, subordinated to capitalist production) by the social changes associated with the rise of capitalism. The English peasantry, for example, was destroyed by forcible eviction from the land and the commercialisation of inputs and outputs, rather than by competition from capitalist farms.

In the early stages of the formation of industrial capital in Britain, the technical methods of production remained largely unchanged. However, the workers lost their direct access to the means of production and the inputs and, therefore, the possibility of controlling their own labour and the output. The process of dispossession of the peasantry, described above, made the wage workers 'free' in two quite distinct senses – free from the lords and the duties imposed by the feudal system, and free from direct access to the means of production. These 'free' workers must sell labour power regularly in order to be able to procure their means of subsistence. Dispossession is one of the key historical sources of the British industrial working class. The other main source is the contracting out of independent artisans to produce goods to order and, later, to process inputs delivered by, and belonging to, a capitalist intermediary (putting out system). The next historical stage was the bringing together of these independent producers to work in 'compounds' belonging to the capitalists, the factories, initially with unchanged technologies (see chapter 3).

The emergence of the factory system is not simply a technological development. It is primarily a process of social reorganisation completing the transformation of independent artisans and dispossessed peasants into wage workers. Marx calls this the *formal subordination* (subsumption) of labour to capital. This choice of terminology highlights the fact that, whereas labour has been effectively subjected to capital, the labour process itself remains essentially unchanged. In this case, exploitation depends primarily upon the extraction of absolute surplus value: the extension of the working day to 12, 14, 16 or more hours per day, the employment of children and the brutal exploitation of every family member for pitiful wages, the disregard for workplace safety and the imposition of degrading living conditions on the working class. Filth, disease, the threat of starvation and the lack of alternatives compelled the 'free' labourers 'voluntarily' to sign up to the labour contract and 'spontaneously' turn up to work even under the most appalling conditions. This is the bedrock of the labour market, a key capitalist institution.

In spite of its humble beginnings, the factory system has profound implications for the organisation of social and individual life. It creates new conditions of labour, and changes the processes of production and social reproduction beyond recognition. Inside each factory, machinery gradually exerts its own discipline. It fragments the labour process into uniform repetitive tasks, which are easily monitored by the agents of capital: the line managers, supervisors, accountants, time-keepers and their hierarchy of superiors, whose own performance is appraised by the board of directors and, ultimately, in developed capitalism, by the firm's banks and shareholders.

Through the processes of mechanisation, labour fragmentation and capitalist control, the factory system transforms the independent artisans and skilled craftspeople into appendages of the machines that they are paid to operate – the factory workers are merely minders of alien fixed capital. Marx calls this the *real subordination* of labour to capital. The detailed co-operation of labour within the factory, and in the economy as a whole, contrasts sharply with its finer division accompanying specialisation. The real subordination of labour marks the beginning of capitalist production proper, based on the extraction of relative surplus value. These are the economic battering rams with which capitalism defeats other forms of production on the basis of its superior efficiency. Simultaneously, outside the factory, towns become rapidly growing industrial centres disrupting every relation between town and country, while life itself is revolutionised by the diffusion of capitalist methods of production throughout the economy, and across the entire world.

Competition and Capital Accumulation

Capitalist competition makes itself felt through different channels. In the sphere of production, competition leads to the real subordination of labour and the extraction of relative surplus value through mechanisation. Institutionally, it is associated with the diffusion of interlocking systems of ownership and control, involving complex hierarchies of 'white collar' workers, managers, executives, shareholders, the financial system and the state, seeking to maximise corporate efficiency often at the expense of the welfare of the workers. Finally, at the level of exchange firms are immersed in competition in several markets simultaneously, including the markets for means of production, labour power and finished commodities. At all levels, capitals find themselves seemingly at the mercy of anonymous 'market forces' – i.e. the imperative of capital in general to accumulate, which determines the behaviour of each individual capital.

In order to distinguish between these channels of competition, and explain their consequences, Marx identifies two distinct types of competition in capitalism: intra-sectoral competition (between capitals in the same branch of industry, producing identical use values), and inter-sectoral competition (between capitals in different branches, producing distinct use values).

Intra-sectoral competition is examined in Volume 1 of *Capital*. This type of competition explains the sources of technical change, the tendency towards the *differentiation* of the profit rates of capitals producing similar goods with distinct technologies, and the possibility of crises of disproportion and overproduction (see chapter 7). When competing against other capitals producing identical commodities, firms can be certain of obtaining average profits (or being able to defend their market share and avoid bankruptcy) only by attempting to become more efficient than the other firms producing the same commodity – that is, unit cost reduction. This requires ruthless discipline and extensive control over the labour process, mechanisation and the continuous introduction of more productive technologies, machines and labour processes, and economies of scale (cost minimisation by large-scale production, reducing average fixed costs).

These continuous upheavals are imposed by systemic imperatives, rather than wickedness or restlessness on the part of the individual capitalist. These forces create a situation of competitive accumulation for all capitalists, the condition of survival being to take part. Competitors will therefore innovate as well as adopt every available technical improvement, eroding the advantage of innovating firms while preserving the incentives for further technical progress across the economy. Fighting this battle increases economic efficiency and cheapens the commodities produced in every firm, farm, shop or office, including those consumed by the workers (relative surplus value). It also tends to strengthen the large capitals, which are normally better able to invest larger sums for longer periods, select among a broader range of production techniques and hire the best workers, which reinforces their initial advantages and, tendentially, destroys their weaker competitors (important counter-tendencies to this process are the diffusion of technical innovations among competing firms, the ability of smaller capitals to undermine the existing technologies through invention and experimentation, and foreign competition).

The second type of competition identified by Marx is inter-sectoral competition, between capitals producing different use values. This type of competition is examined in Volume 3 of *Capital*. It is similar to the market competition between simple commodity producers, which is, however, limited to the sphere of exchange. Rather than leading to the transformation of production technologies and work practices, explained above, profit maximisation can lead instead to capital migration to other (presumably more profitable) sectors. These movements, in response to structural demand shifts, the development of new products or profit opportunities elsewhere, or merely because of short-term repositioning of assets in the stock market, alter the distribution of capital and labour and the productive potential of the economy. Tendentially, they increase supply in the more profitable branches, thus reducing excess profits. An immediate consequence of inter-sectoral competition is the tendency for rates of profit and wages to be *equalised* as economic agents seek maximum exchange value for their commodities on the market. This type of competition also transforms the expression of values as prices, as the latter become prices of production (see chapter 10).

Marx argues that the conflicting forces of competition within and between sectors operate at different levels, with the former being more abstract and relatively more important than the latter. This is because, first, profit must be produced before it can be distributed and tendentially equalised. Second, although migration can raise the profit rate of individual capitals, technical progress can increase the profitability of capital as a whole. Further, in Marx's analysis of the contradictory dynamics of capital accumulation, the conflicting forces unleashed by different types of competition cannot simply be added up, presumably leading to static outcomes, for example relentless concentration of capital through the dispersion of profit rates, or equilibrium with profit rate equalisation, as in mainstream economics. Even if such a state could be reached, it would immediately be disturbed by the relentless pursuit of competitive advantage. Competition is never a smooth process, and it often generates instability and economic crises. For Marx, analysis of competition offers the basis on which more complex structures and processes, influential at different levels and in distinct markets, can be understood.

Capital accumulation is the outcome of the interaction between these two types of competition (both of which are funded by the financial system). A capitalist's ability to compete is clearly limited by the potential to accumulate. Sources of accumulation are twofold. On the one hand, profits may be re-invested, amassing capital over time. Marx called this the process of *concentration*. On the other hand, a capitalist can borrow and merge, gathering the existing resources of capitalist production. This Marx called the process of *centralisation*. Concentration is a slow process diluted by inheritance, but centralisation through the lever of a highly developed credit mechanism and stock markets accomplishes in the twinkling of an eye what would take concentration a hundred years to achieve.

As the individual capitalist accumulates, what is true of each is true of capital as a whole. This is reflected in the social accumulation of capital, the reproduction of capital and its relations of production on an expanded scale, the increase of the proletariat and the development of the forces of production. But the individual capitalist's solution to competition is not reproduced on a social scale: accumulation is also undertaken by competitors so that competition itself is reproduced, both within and between sectors. Competition causes accumulation, accumulation creates competition. Those who fall behind in the accumulation process are destroyed. First it is independent artisans and other modes of production that are swept aside by the advance of productivity, mass production and the iron rule of market evaluation. Later capital turns on itself, big capital destroying little capital as centralisation, credit and concentration amass more and more capital in fewer hands. In sum, capital as self-expanding value exists in rival and separate units, and this mode of existence triggers competition, which is fought by accumulation. The need to accumulate is felt by each individual capitalist as an external coercive force. Accumulate or die: there are few exceptions.

Issues and Further Reading

Marx's study of primitive accumulation in Britain can be found in Marx (1976, part 8). Outstanding studies of the historical origin of capitalism in different regions include Robert Brenner (1986), Terry Byres (1996), Vladimir I. Lenin (1972) and Ellen Wood (1991, 2002); for a critical summary, see Michael Perelman (2003). The origins of capitalism as transition from feudalism have been highly controversial both with and within Marxism. The Dobb–Sweezy debate concerned the relative importance of developments within feudal production and its class relations (as argued for by Dobb) as opposed to the external, disintegrating role of commerce (Sweezy), with corresponding emphases on country and town, and producers and merchants, respectively. The key texts in this debate are included in Rodney Hilton (1976). This controversy has been carried forward by the so-called 'Brenner debate', see Trevor Ashton and Charles Philpin (1985). See also Stephen Marglin (1974) for the idea that the transition to capitalism is initially about how production is organised and ruled rather than in technical methods of production as such.

Marx explains his theory of capitalist reproduction and accumulation in Marx (1976, part 7). The analysis of competition and accumulation in this chapter draws on Ben Fine (1980, chs 2, 6) and Alfredo Saad-Filho (2002, ch. 5); see also Paresh Chattopadhyay (1994, ch. 2), Diego Guerrero (2003), David Harvey (1999, chs 4–7) and John Weeks (1981, ch. 6, 1985–86).

7
Capitalism and Crisis

Capitalism expands because it unleashes economic forces compelling every capital and, to a certain extent, the workers, to behave in ways that are functional for the accumulation of capital as a whole. In spite of this degree of internal coherence, capitalism is also deeply and irredeemably flawed, because the subordination of human needs to the profit motive triggers crises and contradictions that limit the scope for the reproduction of capital. These tensions and limits are discussed below, and reviewed in chapter 14.

Marx's Theory of Accumulation and Crisis

Marx's theory of the necessity as opposed to the possibility of regular crises in capitalist economies draws upon the interaction between competition, class conflicts and the law of the tendency of the rate of profit to fall (LTRPF). The LTRPF will be discussed in chapter 9. For the moment, it is sufficient to observe that crises can occur apart from immediate movements in the rate of profit; indeed, they can be due to factors originating from outside the circuit of capital, for example social, political, financial or technical upheavals. The possibility of erosion in the profit rate because of the inability of capital to 'restructure' to achieve higher profitability, and the fragility of the stock exchange to 'bad' news and its repercussions for economic reproduction, are all too familiar. Other potential causes of crisis include price crashes due to overproduction in key industrial sectors, the collapse of important financial institutions, and instability induced by foreign trade or political turmoil at home.

Marx argues that crises can always arise because of the contradiction between the production of use values for profit and their individual or, more exactly, private consumption. It is only under capitalism, where production for exchange rather than use dominates, that overproduction of a commodity can prove an embarrassment on a social scale. Elsewhere it would be a cause for celebration, because it would mean increased consumption. But for capital, consumption is not enough; sustained accumulation requires the *realisation of profit*. This depends upon sale and, if this becomes impossible, production may be curtailed and capital as a whole forced to operate on a reduced scale.

For example, a set of capitalists producing a particular commodity may be subject to some disturbance generated either in the economic sphere or elsewhere. However, the expanded reproduction of their capitals is intimately integrated with other circuits of capital. Their demands for inputs are other capitalists' supply, and vice versa. The economy may be seen as a system of expanding circuits linked together like interlocking cogwheels. If one set of wheels slows down or grinds to a halt, so may others throughout the system. For example, for the clothing industry to expand there must be a co-ordinated increase in the production of textiles, requiring a higher production of flax and cotton and more machinery, and so on, and more workers and finance must be available for all these industries. It is the necessary but unplanned and competitive interlocking of capitals that leads Marx to talk of the anarchy of capitalist production. In this, Marx anticipates some of Keynes's best insights, not least through his schemes of reproduction. But Marx's analysis goes further and deeper in many respects, extending consideration of the level of (effective) demand to its sources in the production and accumulation of surplus value, and arguing that crises are forcible changes in the pace of accumulation as well as its internal structure. He sees them as *necessary* in the sense that they forcibly resolve the internal contradictions of accumulation which would otherwise persist. Crises are also *unavoidable*, as is shown below.

Possibilities of Crisis

Theories of crisis generally start from the breakdown of an individual circuit of capital, together with the social consequences of private decisions on production and purchase. A circuit of capital may be broken in any of its links (see chapter 5, figure 5.1). The break may be either voluntary or involuntary on the part of the capitalist, being able but unwilling or willing but unable to allow the circuit to continue. In the first case the capitalist will be speculating. Either the capitalist is anticipating that profitability may be increased by delaying the circuit, or hoping to create or exploit a monopoly position by doing so. In the second case, the capitalist is subject to forces beyond immediate control.

There is unlikely to be a break of the circuit in the sphere of production, unless labour takes industrial action or there are major natural or technical disruptions (including rapid technological change in unfavourable financial circumstances). Almost all crises will appear to originate in the sphere of circulation as an inability or unwillingness to buy, sell or invest. Consider the arm $M - C<^{MP}_{LP}$. A voluntary break here implies that C is available for sale, but the owner of the M might anticipate a lower price for the inputs or hope to create such a lower price. In particular, for the labour input, this may be done by reducing (or threatening to reduce) the level of employment as part of a strategy to increase the rate of surplus value.

The break in the circuit could also be involuntary. The owners of the inputs may attempt to create or exploit a 'monopoly' position – in particular, labour may strike. Alternatively, inputs may not be available because, in the previous round of social production, outputs – partly present inputs – may have been produced in the wrong proportions. This will provide for an excess demand of a particular commodity and normally an excess supply in some other sector. If this situation becomes generalised across many producers and sectors, the situation is termed a crisis of disproportionality. These remarks need to be modified if the commodity in short supply is labour power. Then there will be an excess demand for labour but also an excess supply of (unused) money capital.

A break in the sphere of circulation may also appear between C' and M'. A capitalist may speculate about the future price of commodity capital, in case of a voluntary break. Alternatively, it may be impossible to sell produce.

This means the commodity is in excess supply. This could be because of disproportionality or because those who normally buy the commodity may be unable to do so because they do not have money to hand, access to credit or profitable prospects. For example, if other circuits have been broken, for whatever reason, workers, capitalists and others will not receive their regular flow of money income and hence will not make a regular flow of money expenditures. If this last situation becomes generalised, it is known as a crisis of underconsumption (or, from another point of view, overproduction). Marx put the whole matter neatly when he suggested that commodities are in love with money but the course of true love never did run smooth.

Marxists have usually looked at crises of underconsumption/overproduction and disproportionality by dividing the economy into two sectors, investment and consumption, following Marx's scheme for expanded reproduction (see chapter 5). Some have argued that there is a persistent tendency for the supply of consumption goods to outstrip the demand for them, others that the tendency exists for a disproportionately large production of investment goods. Both are logically possible, but disproportions – overproduction in one sector, underproduction in another – are just as likely to occur within the consumption and investment goods sectors as between the two as aggregates. In all this, it is possible to confuse a crisis of disproportionality in which consumption goods are in excess supply with a crisis of underconsumption. The latter will be characterised by a general overproduction of commodities and the simultaneous development of excess industrial capacity, which must be generated by some exogenous disturbance. A crisis of disproportionality does not presuppose these exogenous influences but may itself be one, tending to generate a crisis of underconsumption.

Breaks in individual circuits of capital will occur infinitely often given the anarchy of capitalist production, fluctuations in market prices, the vagaries of the credit system, speculation, monopolisation and the economic obsolescence of fixed capital with technological progress. Occasionally these will be sufficiently important to generate a crisis, its extent depending upon the pattern of adjustment in economic reproduction. However, this description of the possibilities of crisis is limited because it leaves aside the motive of capitalist production: profit. The most important factor from the capitalist's standpoint is the amount of profit thrown off by the circuit of capital. All obstacles to the circuit's movement may be overcome if *s* is large enough. Should profitability be improving, capitalists will be reluctant to speculate on higher and later profit, deny wage increases, or in any way hinder the process of profit-making. This is so much so that the financial system will often prolong a speculative boom long after profitability has begun to decline in anything other than paper terms. This can temper the frequency of crises even if at the expense of deepening those that do occur. As a result, a potential source of crisis is more than likely to be insignificant, given sufficient profitability. Profits can pay and pave the way.

However, should the ability to expand the production of profit be constrained, then not only will some capitalists be expelled from production by bankruptcy, but general pessimism will reign, production will be curtailed, and a crisis will be generated. Movements in profitability depend not only on the conditions of sale, but also on movements in values. As has been seen in chapter 3, the process of competitive accumulation brings frequent reductions in the values of all commodities. It is a contradictory feature of capitalism that individual profit is pursued by reducing values through relative expulsion of living labour from production, even though labour is the source of surplus value. Marx analyses this in the context of the law of the tendency of the rate of profit to fall (see chapter 9).

Theories of crisis due to overproduction, underconsumption, disproportionality and the falling rate of profit have given rise to an extensive literature; however, in isolation these approaches are limited. Rather than being presented as competing Marxian crisis theories in their own right, they can be more usefully analysed as aspects of Marx's crisis theory.

Intra-sectoral competition (see chapter 6) creates a tendency toward uneven (disproportional) industrial development between sectors, and overproduction within them. In certain circumstances, possibly associated with a decline in the profit rate, these processes may trigger a general crisis. However, more important than these associations is the fundamental cause of crisis. For Marx, capitalist crises are due to the contradiction between the capitalist tendency to develop without limit the productive forces (and the surplus value that has to be realised), and the limited social capacity to consume the product. Economic stability under these circumstances requires that an increasing part of the product must be purchased by capitalists for investment purposes, which is not always possible. Capitalism is therefore increasingly prone to crisis. The crisis explodes when production has developed beyond the possibility of profitable realisation. This can occur for different reasons, and what matters for the explanation of specific crises is how their underlying cause – the subordination of the production of use values to the production of surplus value – manifests itself through disproportionality, overproduction, underconsumption and the falling rate of profit.

Accumulation, Crisis and the Development of the Proletariat

Suppose that as capital accumulates the ratio between constant and variable capital advanced (c/v) remains unchanged. If the real wage is also unchanged, the employment of labour must increase. It would be unrealistic to expect that the labour supply can be increased indefinitely without an increase in wages. However, if the wage rate increases faster than productivity in the wage goods sector there will be a squeeze on profitability and, tendentially, a reduction in the rate of accumulation (in the limit, there will be no accumulation of capital when wages approach such a level that the production of any surplus value at all is threatened). Yet as accumulation slackens so does the demand for labour, and the upward pressure on the wage rate is reduced as labour's power diminishes with unemployment. Profitability is restored, and with it accumulation, and the cycle repeats itself (this argument has to be qualified should the ratio c/v change, see chapter 8).

This is how Marx characterised the decennial business cycles observed in the early nineteenth century. He also linked them to the synchronised renewal of fixed capital and the volatility of commercial credit. In contrast to Classical political economists, he explained fluctuations in employment by fluctuations in the rate of accumulation and its effects on wages and profitability (rather than vice versa). He considered absurd the Malthusian doctrine of alternating decimation and stimulation of the size of the proletariat by sexual reproduction in response to wages below and then above subsistence. This could hardly explain ten-year cycles. Marx was also heavily critical of the Classical economists, who were spellbound by the idea of decreasing returns in agricultural production (see chapter 13). In contrast, he stressed the productivity of capital. Described in these aggregate terms, economic activity, determined by changes in the rate of accumulation, appears to fluctuate smoothly. Nothing could be further from the truth. The overall picture may conceal enormous variations between sectors of production and geographic regions within a capitalist economy. Moreover, it has already been shown that capital has a tendency to increase productivity and expel living labour from the production process.

Marx argues that, under capitalism, technical change would not only save living labour absolutely, but also relative to other means of production. This is achieved by the economies of scale due to factories and the use of new machinery. Thus there will be an increase in the amount of machinery per worker, which increases the technical composition of capital (see chapter 8) as well as speeding up the production process. Each worker turns over a given mass of raw materials in a shorter time, reducing the amount of labour socially necessary to produce each commodity.

The expulsion of living labour from production may be accompanied by an overall expansion in employment, because of the rapid growth of the total output.

Competitive accumulation, however, proceeds in an uncoordinated fashion. Across sectors and regions, outputs and employment will not expand in balanced proportions. With the technological changes there will now be a shortage, now an excess of labour and means of production available. However, the expulsion of living labour from *all* production processes will tend to produce a continuous flow of labour into unemployment to form a surplus population (tempered, as explained above, by economic expansion and the opening of new sectors and avenues for accumulation). Marx called this the *industrial reserve army*, or *surplus population* – note that the surplus is created by capital accumulation, rather than the biological reproduction of the workers as in Malthus. Among these there will be a layer of permanently unemployed, condemned to pauperisation by the combination of the rhythm and characteristics of accumulation, and their own perceived unsuitability for capitalist employment, whether it be because of age, gender, past experiences (or lack thereof) or disability. The greater is the reserve army relative to employment, the greater is the competition for employment and the lower will be wages. But the greater is the absolute size of the reserve army and its layer of permanently unemployed, the greater is the extension of poverty and misery. Marx singled out this feature of capitalism as the *general law of capitalist accumulation*.

So far, we have analysed the demands that capital accumulation places on the proletariat – a constant disruption of individual and social life. Particular changes may be forced by political, economic, ideological and legal coercion, or induced through the market by changes in wages and skill requirements. The particular method chosen and the outcome will depend upon the strength of organisation behind the two classes. In addition the strength of the capitalist class increases as accumulation is accompanied by greater centralisation and, simultaneously, by the greater strength, organisation and coercive power of the state. Marx argues that, at the same time as capital is centralised, so are masses of workers concentrated together in production. Social organisation encourages their political awareness and economic activity, which increases their influence on political life. As accumulation progresses, so the strength, organisation and discipline of the proletariat grow with the development of its material conditions.

Capitalism fulfils the positive role of developing society's productive potential, turns the principles of economic efficiency into universally held values, and creates the material conditions for communism. Yet, at the same time capitalism is the most *destructive* mode of production in history. Capitalist economies are chronically unstable because of the conflicting forces of extraction, realisation and accumulation of surplus value under competitive conditions. This instability is structural, and even the best economic policies cannot avoid it completely. It was shown in chapter 6 that competition forces every capital to find ways to increase labour productivity. This generally involves technical changes that increase the degree of mechanisation, the integration between labour processes within and across firms, and the potential scale of production. But these processes are always uneven and wasteful. They are associated with large fixed capital investment, speculation, labour market shifts, deskilling, structural unemployment, bankruptcy, crisis and the creation of unsatisfied and basic needs in spite of the ready availability of the means to avoid them.

Accumulation also contributes to the development of the agent of capital's destruction, the organised workers, and the rationale for that destruction: the socialisation of consumption to be accomplished by a socially co-ordinated plan harnessing society's productive potential. The proletariat accomplishes its historical role, expropriation of the class of capitalists, when capitalist society can no longer provide the conditions that labour requires of it. This does not necessarily occur during an economic crisis. For while crises are associated with reduced profits, high unemployment and downward pressures on wages, a recession is also a time when the working class tends to be weakened. In addition, changes within a mode of production, let alone the transition from one to another, cannot simply be read off from economic conditions alone, because they are highly dependent on political and ideological conditions. These, together with the labour movement's economic position, tend to be at their strongest when conditions are prosperous. So the relationship between economic analysis and revolution is not only complex, but is dependent upon other influences as well (this is explored further in chapter 14).

Issues and Further Reading

The literature on crisis theory is extensive, diverse and bitterly contested. One division is between those who hold to a theory of falling profitability (and there are differences between them over how and why) and those who do not. Other differences in the literature reflect relative emphasis on production, distribution, exchange, finance and the balance of power between capital and labour and within the capitalist class. Increasingly, the (economic) role of the state has been seen as a source of, or response to, crisis, although this now has less prominence in deference to 'globalisation'.

Marx himself never discusses his theory of crisis systematically; see, however, Karl Marx (1969, ch. 17 and 1972, ch. 20). The interpretation in this chapter is based on Ben Fine and Laurence Harris (1979, ch. 5). For overviews of Marx's theory of crisis, see Simon Clarke (1994), Duncan Foley (1986, ch. 9), David Harvey (1999, ch. 13), Michael Howard and John King (1990), Michael Perelman (1987), Anwar Shaikh (1978), John Weeks (1981, chs 5, 8) and *Research in Political Economy* (vol. 18, 2000). Underconsumptionist theories are critically reviewed by Michael Bleaney (1976) and John Weeks (1982b). A renewal of the debate has been sparked by Robert Brenner (1998, 2002). For a taste of the ensuing literature, see *Historical Materialism* (vols 4–5, 1999) and Ben Fine, Costas Lapavitsas and Dimitris Milonakis (1999).

8
The Compositions of Capital

This chapter explains Marx's concepts of technical, organic and value compositions of capital, as a prelude to the study of the law of the tendency of the rate of profit to fall (LTRPF) and the transformation problem, in chapters 9 and 10. This is important for two reasons. First, although the compositions of capital are essential for understanding the relationship between values and prices, technical change, economic crises and other structures and processes in the capitalist economy, they have been generally explained cursorily and understood only superficially and incorrectly in the literature. Second, the LTRPF is traditionally seen as having only a passing relationship with the transformation problem. This is incorrect, for they are closely related to one another through the composition of capital. This is explained in detail below.

The Technical Composition of Capital

In Volume 1 of *Capital* Marx examines the specifically capitalist method of production, i.e. the systematic way in which capitalism seizes and transforms the labour process in creating the factory system, and appropriates the other conditions of production, for example, the natural resources (see chapters 6 and 14). In Volume 1 Marx also establishes the tendency for the productivity of labour to rise systematically under capitalism through raising the mass of means of production that is worked up into final commodities in a given labour time. This process is captured by the concept of the technical composition of capital (TCC).

The TCC is the physical ratio between the material inputs used up and the living labour necessary to transform them into the output. Although Marx shows that the TCC tends to rise (this being the expression of the rising productivity of labour under capitalism), attempts to measure the TCC and its changes, or to contrast the technical composition of capitals in different sectors (e.g. agriculture and shipbuilding) face a severe problem: the TCC cannot be measured directly, because it is the ratio between a heterogeneous bundle of use values (the material inputs) and quantities of concrete labour spent in each firm or sector. In other words, the TCC can be measured by a single index only in so far as a mass of heterogeneous raw materials and living labour are reduced to a common denominator.

For mainstream theory, the measurement of the TCC is an index number problem. In contrast, in Marx's theory the value of commodities forms the basis on which the TCC can be appropriately measured. This is not simply the choice of one index rather than another. It reflects Marx's proposition that value, understood as socially necessary labour time, is a legitimate category of analysis for a capitalist society. In this society, as was shown in chapter 2, different concrete labours are regularly, systematically and necessarily brought into equivalence with each other in production as well as exchange, thereby establishing the dominance of value relations within capitalism. Value measurements of the TCC are legitimate (rather than simply convenient, with the drawbacks associated with any index number) because they express the systematic changes in the conditions of production under capitalism, in terms of the social and value relations in which they are embodied. In other words, the measurement of the TCC by values is not a more or less convenient and arbitrary index of changing production conditions, but a conceptualisation of part of the accumulation process.

The Organic and Value Compositions

These comments are borne out when the ways of constructing the value measure of the TCC are analysed in further detail. Close reading of *Capital* shows that, in addition to the technical composition, Marx distinguishes between the *organic* and *value* compositions of capital (OCC and VCC). However, the OCC and VCC have rarely been distinguished in the literature, and the two have often been used almost interchangeably. For both, the algebraic definition has generally been denoted by c/v (constant divided by variable capital). However, this begs the question: what values are being used to reduce the heterogeneous bundle of raw materials, in the case of c, and of living labour, in the case of v, to single value dimensions? This is a pertinent problem in this context, since the whole analysis is concerned with accumulation and, therefore, with the systematic reduction in the values of commodities through technical change (see chapter 3).

Before dealing with this problem in the dynamic context of accumulation, it is useful for expositional purposes to distinguish the VCC and the OCC in a static context. Consider, for example, the production of jewellery. Suppose that exactly the same labour process and the same machines and technology are used to produce both silver and gold rings. Both production processes will have the same TCC, since this measures the mass of raw materials relative to living labour. But the production of gold rings will involve a higher VCC since it uses raw materials of a higher value (gold as opposed to silver). To reflect the lack of difference in the production processes from the technical point of view, Marx defines the OCC as *equal* for the two production processes. In other words, the OCC measures the TCC in value terms, but *leaving aside* the differences created by the greater or lesser value of the raw materials employed.

This creates some difficulty in measuring the OCC, since the appropriate values at which to define the ratio of *c* to *v* are not specified. Should we, for example, use the value of gold, the value of silver or something in between for the definition? This is a problem created by the attempt to make the distinction in a static context. It is only when production processes are changing that the distinction between the OCC and the VCC has any real significance, for otherwise the TCC and the VCC alone are adequate to specify the equivalence or otherwise between production processes from the organic point of view.

Consider now a dynamic example, involving the steel industry. Suppose that, because of technical improvements in this industry, there is a reduction in the value of steel. As a result, the VCC in every sector of the economy will change according to the relative content of steel in the production of its constant capital and in the value of labour power. In a simpler case, with a homogeneous labour force employed in all sectors, the VCCs will vary according to the relative use of steel. In spite of this change, the OCCs in all sectors will remain unchanged, because there has been no change in the TCCs. This example shows that the OCC measures changes in production in value terms, and so it can measure something distinct from the VCC only when the TCC is changing. Obviously, the two examples given above only serve to explain the difference between the VCC and the OCC. They do not have much significance in themselves.

The matter is different once we begin to consider changing conditions of production. Marx argues that, at its developed stage, capitalism involves accumulation through the production of relative surplus value, with machinery systematically displacing living labour. This results in a tendency towards a rising TCC across the economy. In this case, the TCC can be measured in value terms in two different ways.

On the one hand, from the point of view of changes in production alone, the TCC is measured by the OCC. Raw materials and labour power enter the production process with given values, and this leads to a definite ratio of constant to variable capital, according to the extent to which labour is coerced to transform inputs into outputs. If we were to put it chronologically, the OCC measures the TCC at the 'old' values prevailing prior to the technical changes and the renewal of the production process. On the other hand, whenever there is technical progress somewhere in the economy there is a change (reduction) in the values of commodities. The VCC is measured at this stage. Necessarily, it takes account of the TCC from the point of view of the change both in the OCC and in the values of commodities as they are realised in the sphere of exchange. To put it chronologically, the VCC is measured at the 'new' rather than at the 'old' values. In sum, the VCC captures the contradictory implications of the rising TCC as well as the falling values due to technological progress – therefore, the VCC tends to rise more slowly than the TCC and the OCC.

The description of the difference between the VCC and the OCC in terms of new and old values is slightly misleading, since the distinction is conceptual rather than chronological: at any moment in time some capitals will be entering the production process as others will be leaving it; moreover, technical change is ubiquitous. What the distinction does is to draw upon, and build in a more complex context, the separation between the spheres of production and exchange (see chapter 4). In production, the two classes of capitalists and workers confront each other over the process of production and, as accumulation proceeds, there is a tendency for the TCC to rise. In exchange, capitalists confront each other as competitors in the process of buying and selling and, as accumulation proceeds, there is a tendency for values to be reduced, and for the VCC to decline.

It is shown in the next chapter that the interaction of these processes, as understood in the structural separation between production and exchange, is the concern of Marx's LTRPF. In chapter 10, the relationship between values and prices in Marx is explained through the role of the OCC in his value analysis.

Issues and Further Reading

As mentioned, the literature has been careless over treatment of the compositions of capital. Generally, in the context of the LTRPF, most attention has been focused, at least in terminology, upon the OCC, with scant regard for the TCC and VCC. Ironically, despite the terminological predominance of the OCC, the VCC has been what has been meant in practice. This reflects disregard for Marx's own distinctions and misinterpretation of his work and intent.

Not surprisingly, the literature specifically on the compositions of capital is scant. Marx explains his concepts in Karl Marx (1969, ch. 12, 1972, ch. 23, and 1981a, ch. 8). The interpretation in this chapter draws upon Ben Fine (1990a) and Ben Fine and Laurence Harris (1979, ch. 4). This interpretation is reviewed and developed in the light of the existing literature by Alfredo Saad-Filho (1993, 2001 and 2002, ch. 6).

9
The Falling Rate of Profit

Marx's theory of the law of the tendency of the rate of profit to fall (LTRPF) has been extremely controversial in terms of its validity, interpretation and significance. This chapter outlines Marx's law and answers some of the criticisms that have been levelled against it. Two misguided interpretations of the LTRPF are often found in the literature. On the one hand, Marx's contribution is removed to the realm of high philosophy, in which the LTRPF takes on the character of an abstract truth, something derived from the logic of capital itself and therefore irrefutable. On the other hand, Marx's analysis has been treated as if it amounted to a set of algebraic propositions that are correct, incorrect or somewhere in between, depending on the analyst's inclinations and the algebraic implications of the chosen model of the economy.

The position adopted here differs from both of these, admittedly parodied, extremes. However, the argument is a complex one, depending upon conceptual rather than algebraic considerations. As a result, the structure of the analysis is summarised first and is followed by a more detailed account containing elaboration and justification.

Summary of the Argument

Marx's LTRPF is based upon the conceptual distinction between the organic and value compositions of capital (OCC and VCC), with the literature rarely distinguishing between the two and generally using the term OCC when referring to the VCC. In chapter 8, it was shown that the OCC measures the results of accumulation by exclusive reference to the sphere of *production*, i.e. (surplus) value creation, whilst the VCC measures and reflects the process of accumulation in the sphere of *exchange*, i.e. (surplus) value realisation, which centres on but should not be confined to the problem of sale.

The OCC tends to rise over time because of the adoption of specifically capitalist methods of production, especially the use of machinery in the context of competition within sectors and the systematic attempt to extract relative surplus value. This tendency of the OCC to increase is the source of the law as such, whilst the formation of the VCC is associated with the counteracting tendencies (CTs) to the LTRPF. The interaction between the law and the CTs is an essential underlying aspect of the process of capital accumulation. Their interaction forms more complex economic phenomena, but only for that stage of development of capitalism for which machine production is predominant.

This implies that the LTRPF is not an empirical law in the narrowly predictive sense – it is, rather, an *abstract law* that does not give prospective indications about movements in the rate of profit. However, it provides the basis on which more complex and immediate economic phenomena can be studied by the inclusion of further logical and historical analysis (see chapter 1).

This presentation of Marx's LTRPF leads to a complete contrast with the understanding and criticism of it associated with the Japanese economist Nobuo Okishio, which has been taken up by the Sraffian school of economics, as well as by some Marxists. Because this approach is limited to comparative statics and equilibrium analysis, it treats the accumulation process as one that necessarily engenders a harmonious interaction between production and circulation. Consequently, this approach can be characterised as the dialectical opposite of Marx's.

The Law as Such and the Counteracting Tendencies

Marx's treatment of the LTRPF occupies the three chapters of the third part of Volume 3 of *Capital.* The first chapter is entitled 'The Law Itself'. It contains what appears to be a simple algebraic demonstration of falling profitability in capitalism. Since the rate of profit may, in value terms, be written as $r = s/(c+v) = e/(\text{OCC} + 1)$ where e is the rate of surplus value (s/v) and the OCC is c/v, a fall in r is immediate from the rising OCC, provided there is no rise in e.

However, this interpretation is incorrect. The LTRPF does not predict empirical movements in the rate of profit, for two reasons. First, Marxian laws are not the theoretical expression of empirical regularities. Here, an analogy with the law of gravity might help. It is based upon the idea that bodies mutually attract one another as in Newton's apple falling to the earth. But, empirically, the law of gravity *explains* empirical outcomes that appear to contradict it as a law – planets traverse stable orbits around the sun and buildings remain upright. Similarly, Marxian laws express the key material forces constituted by capitalist social relations, what Marx calls tendencies. This is why the LTRPF is seemingly oddly named 'law of the tendency'. Although Marxian laws and tendencies arise from the social relations defining the mode of production, and they are therefore necessary (unavoidable), they do not directly determine empirical outcomes. For example, the tendency towards mechanisation and the rising OCC does not imply that the profit rate must drop like a stone; conversely, fluctuations of the profit rate over time do not negate the LTRPF. By the same token, the tendency for profit rate equalisation across sectors as a result of profit maximisation and capital mobility does not imply that these rates will (or even might) be equalised in the future (it is only in mainstream economics that this tendency is seen as an actuality, so that an equilibrium can be constructed in which all profit rates are equalised).

For Marx, laws and tendencies have to be located analytically in the context of their sources and the more complex ways in which they manifest themselves. For example, tendencies always interact with counter-tendencies as well as in the context of particular historical circumstances, leading to undetermined – but, in principle, understandable – outcomes (see chapter 1). In the case of competing capitals, for example, the tendency for their profit rates to be equalised has to be set against the competition between capitals in the same sector, which differentiates their rates of profit from the average, whether this be through accumulation to increase productivity, the paying of lower wages, or whatever (see chapter 6).

The second reason why the LTRPF does not permit empirical predictions is that any consideration of the organic (rather than value) composition of capital, as is the case in this law, is restricted to changes in production without any reference to value changes in circulation. This explains why the constant value of *e* is not an arbitrary assumption but, rather, an expression of the unchanging values of commodities (including labour power) during production.

Marx's second chapter, entitled 'Counteracting Factors', deals with the CTs. These fall into two types. There are those that follow directly from the changes in values resulting from the rising OCC. If we write $r = s/(c+v)$, it follows that anything that reduces *c* or *v*, and anything that increases *s*, tends to increase *r*. The production of relative surplus value does all of these, because the increase in productivity implies a reduction in the value of *c* and *v* (whether directly in the wage goods sector or indirectly through its use of lower valued raw materials) and an increase in *s*, through the reduction of *v* (given the real wage). These changes in the values of commodities are synonymous with the formation of the VCC, as previously argued, highlighting the importance of this concept and its difference with the OCC.

In addition, Marx also considers CTs of a less systematic variety, which do not follow directly from capital accumulation. For example, he lists the super-exploitation of the workforce (absolute surplus value), the cheapening of raw materials and wage goods through foreign trade, and the formation of joint stock companies. This group of CTs does not follow of necessity from capital accumulation or the rising OCC, even though they are results of capitalist development. Marx appears to lump them together with the others without separating them analytically. This may be explained by the lack of final preparation of Volume 3 for publication. In addition, Marx's list of CTs follows closely that of J.S. Mill, suggesting that he had yet to rework his material properly. However, an important difference between Marx and Mill is that the latter's treatment of the law follows that of Ricardo, and is based upon the *declining productivity of agriculture*, rather than, as with Marx, the *increasing productivity across all industry.*

This treatment of the CTs by Marx makes it appear as though he is dealing with immediate movements in *r* as a numerical counterweight to the law as such. However, the CTs are certainly presented at a more complex level of analysis than the law, for, as we have seen, they involve the formation of the VCC, which incorporates changes both in production *and* exchange (whereas the law itself involves the formation of the OCC, and changes in production only). In spite of this, like the law, the CTs should not be seen as factors of empirical weight directly governing movements in the rate of profit, but as embodying those processes that transform the changing conditions of production into movements in exchange.

The Internal Contradictions of the Law

In the previous section we have interpreted both the LTRPF and the CTs as capturing relatively abstract processes and relations rather than as predicting immediate movements in the rate of profit. This is the basis on which to examine Marx's third chapter on the LTRPF, aptly named 'Development of the Law's Internal Contradictions'. In this chapter, he examines the law and the CTs as a contradictory unity of underlying processes giving rise to more complex empirical phenomena. Even at this relatively concrete stage, Marx is more concerned with the antagonistic co-existence of the law and its CTs than with the prediction of movements in the rate of profit. This is because the law and the CTs cannot be added together algebraically to give a rise or fall in the rate of profit according to which of the two happens to be the stronger. Rather, Marx is concerned with the contradictions between the production and circulation of (surplus) value as the process of value creation proceeds on the basis of existing values, even as these are reduced by the accumulation of capital.

The fact that the LTRPF concerns the interaction of abstract tendencies, rather than anticipating a relentless decline in the actual profit rates of capitalist firms or economies, is implicitly confirmed by Marx's analysis of the internal contradictions of the law. There is little or no discussion of movements in the rate of profit in the third part of Volume 3 of *Capital*, and a much greater concern with the ability of the economy to accumulate the mass of surplus value that it has been able to produce, and needs in order to expand. In other words, there is a greater focus on whether accumulation can be sustained than on whether it generates a higher or lower rate of profit. For example, if technical progress reduces the values of constant and variable capital, as it tends to do, this is indicative of the translation of changes in conditions of production into the sphere of exchange, and it generates a tendency towards falling profit rates (to the extent that the value of labour power is sustained, and real wages increase, in line with accumulation and productivity). In contrast, the formation of joint stock companies, the super-exploitation of the workers and the opening up of foreign trade are conducive to a continuing accumulation irrespective of the rate of profit at which they occur.

The Empirical Implications of the Law

The consideration of the LTRPF as an abstract law does not deny its empirical significance. Marx's main conclusion in this part of *Capital* is that the law and CTs cannot exist side by side in harmony indefinitely, but must at times give rise to crises. This requires careful interpretation, for there is no axiomatic derivation of the necessity of crises, just as there is no axiomatic derivation of a falling rate of profit. Rather, Marx is pointing to the *immanent* possibility of crises, just as he had previously done so in Volume 2, as a result of the narrower potential of disjuncture between sale and purchase on the basis of unchanging values (see chapter 7).

For the LTRPF, a potential source of disjuncture is the accommodation in exchange of the relative expulsion of labour and the changing values in production. These processes of accommodation are subject to incessant disruption because of technical change throughout the economy. For example, the reduction in values as accumulation proceeds tends to undermine the preservation of existing values and their embodiment in capital, while the expulsion of labour disrupts the balances between supply and demand and the reproduction of labour power. These disturbances demonstrate that the LTRPF and the counteracting tendencies have a connection with observable phenomena even though they do not involve simple predictions of trends. However, they provide a framework for understanding the tensions and displacements due to capital accumulation, and they support the conclusion that the law and the CTs cannot co-exist side by side in repose even during a phase of expansion: capitals are being devalued even as they are being preserved and expanded. The existence of these contradictions gives rise to crises, booms and the associated cycles of production and exchange. Moreover, the development of the immanent possibility of crisis points to the *likelihood* of crisis when these processes can no longer be accommodated, especially (but not exclusively) because of disproportions, misguided investment and speculative bubbles. These crises, and the resulting unemployment, concentration and centralisation of capital, and so on, are the observable 'predictions' of Marx's abstract tendency. Indeed, particular movements in the observable rate of profit are associated with these cycles. At times the rate of profit will actually fall, at others it will rise. These movements are not arbitrary but are based on the abstract tendencies and their contradictions.

This analysis leads to *further* empirical implications of the LTRPF, for it suggests that crises that owe their origins to developments in the sphere of production will, nevertheless, break in the sphere of circulation, and may do so in surprising ways, depending on the relative strengths and fragilities of the participants in the circuit of capital as a whole. This is one reason why the LTRPF is liable to lead empirically to actual falls in the rate of profit: as the accumulation process falters, the mass of profit realised is set against an unchanging mass of fixed capital, so that profitability tends to decline. But this need not be so. If, for example, as a result of economic stagnation or bankruptcies large masses of capital are depreciated or bought up by surviving capitalists at rock bottom prices, the rate of profit may even rise as a result of the crisis (this process often plays an important role in economic recovery).

LTRPF and Crisis Theory

The previous point illustrates that the falling rate of profit has been something of a fetish in the literature, whatever the position adopted in relation to Marx's own analysis. The focus has been on whether or not theory can produce a fall in the rate of profit, by whatever mechanism, whether it be a rising OCC, VCC or wages (at the expense of profits). Once the rate of profit falls, it is presumed that the economy collapses into crisis because of deficient investment leading, in turn, to deficient demand for potential output as in Keynesian theory. In this perspective, there is a complete separation between the theory that yields the fall in profitability and the results of that fall, i.e. between the cause and the course of the crisis (and, at a further remove, the recovery mechanism – which, in Keynes's analysis, depends upon a *deus ex machina*, state deficit spending and its impact upon capitalist expectations). However, it cannot be presumed that a fall in profitability automatically results in a crisis. There may be a reduced incentive and capacity to accumulate in terms of reward, but some reward is better than none. Continuing accumulation may be necessary to preserve existing (fixed) capital, repay existing debts and, most important of all, falling profitability acts as a powerful competitive force. Consequently, as capitalists attempt to restore profitability, they may even accumulate at a faster rate than previously!

For Marx, the generation of crises through proximate falls in the rate of profit is a possibility (e.g. industrial bankruptcies leading to bank failures and a credit crunch), but this does not offer a penetrating analysis of the general cause and course of crises. More importantly, it does not demonstrate the organic relationship between the crisis and the process of capital accumulation except trivially, by implying that an unco-ordinated market economy is unable to achieve long-term balanced growth. In contrast, if the LTRPF is understood as the combination of contradictory tendencies uniting production and exchange, then the examination of these tendencies, at the more complex level of their interaction, opens the way to an analysis of crises linked to and based upon the *accumulation process*.

This requires an analysis of value production and formation in exchange in a much wider context than is presented in the opening chapters of Volume 1 of *Capital*. There, the category of value is understood as a social relation that expresses the real equivalence between different types of concrete labour, through the category of abstract labour. In every economy, there will inevitably be different skills of labour as well as different types of labour. Within each sector, there will also be different levels of productivity across the competing firms. But the profit imperative, competition within and between sectors, capitalist control over the labour process, and commodity equivalence in exchange forcibly reduce these labours to the common denominator of value (see chapters 2 and 3).

With accumulation and the competition to reduce commodity values, socially necessary labour time (SNLT) in each sector becomes the centre around which individual labour and accumulation processes revolve.

Recognition of the interaction between the law and the CTs raises difficult problems for value theory, which can be resolved only through a more complex and concrete understanding of value. For example, since accumulation leads to a reduction in SNLT the whole concept of value appears to be at risk, for we are attempting to utilise a category whose quantification is upset as soon as it is established. The only way to address this difficulty is through the recognition that the equivalence established between different types of labour is extended through time to labours of different productivity. We have already illustrated two instances of this process. First, inputs manufactured at different points in time, and with different technologies, are combined and transformed by living labour into new output which, in turn, is often consumed productively as an input in another production process. As such, the material equivalence between different types of labour and between labours of different productivity is established in production rather than exchange. Second, the OCC is constructed on the basis of equivalence for previously established values, whereas the VCC is formed through the process of re-establishing values in the wake of the changing production conditions associated with the rising OCC.

This is as much as one can say about the dynamics of the general profit rate at this level of analysis, and no further progress can be made without specifying the nature of the interaction between the law and the CTs. This can be done theoretically, by extending the analysis of the mechanisms by which value relations are expressed in exchange, or empirically, by specifying the conditions in which accumulation takes place historically. Two important factors in both aspects of the analysis of profitability are the role of finance and the role of fixed capital. In their own different ways, both are hugely influential in, and directly affected by, the establishment of value equivalence in exchange as values are changing. They are most problematic in a world of changing values, in which capitals seek to preserve and pass on value over an extended period, during which they are liable to be competitively confronted by cheaper substitutes and more productive competitors. These topics cannot be taken up here, but see chapter 3 and further readings.

A Response to Okishio

The best-known criticism of Marx's theory of the LTRPF takes as its point of departure a theorem presented by the Japanese economist Nobuo Okishio. Briefly and informally, Okishio argued that, given a wider availability of techniques of production, the rate of profit cannot fall unless real wages rise. In other words, a falling rate of profit is contingent upon rising wages, rather than being the result of contradictions in the process of capital accumulation, as was shown above to be the case for Marx. In Okishio's analysis, new techniques of production become available to capitalists, who adopt them if and only if they are more profitable than the existing techniques, given the prevailing commodity prices. Once these new techniques are generalised across the sectors concerned, this will result in a new (lower) set of prices and a new rate of profit, equalised across sectors. Of course, prices will change not only in the sectors where there has been innovation, because these presumably lower prices will be passed on to the sectors in which those commodities are used as inputs or as part of the wage. In this case, Okishio's question is the following: could the capitalists, acting blindly to increase individual profitability by introducing new techniques, paradoxically lead the system to a lower rate of profit? Not surprisingly, he comes up with a negative answer, unless real wages are increased, and concludes that Marx is incorrect.

To begin with, it is important to recognise that Okishio's theorem is an exercise in comparative statics, i.e. it compares one position of economic equilibrium with another. This use of comparative statics is clearly inappropriate in the context of the analysis of movements in the rate of profit as a source of crises. In other words, if we move from one equilibrium to another, we cannot be analysing crises whatever happens to the rate of profit. There is only one exception to this argument, discussed in the previous section and shown to be of limited relevance and validity, which is if the movements in the rate of profit are independent from, but the source of, subsequent crises. Here, however, Okishio comes up with the result that, first, the economy moves from one position of static equilibrium to another. Second, implicitly, if the rate of profit falls, we have a crisis, but otherwise we do not. It is left unclear, however, why the equilibrium, even with a lower rate of profit, would suddenly collapse into crisis.

This raises the much more interesting question of the movement between the two equilibria. By examining this process, it is apparent that, far from interpreting Marx's LTRPF, the approach associated with Okishio is its dialectical opposite. For, in Okishio's approach, an individual capitalist initially adopts a more advantageous technique of production, whether through superior access to finance or technology and, at the initial prices, this capitalist makes a higher than average rate of profit. Although this conclusion is correct, in the narrow sense of Okishio's problem, this approach contrasts sharply with Marx's analysis of the rising OCC. For Marx, as was shown above, the tendency for falling profitability is due to the evaluation of inputs and outputs at old values, and it holds for *capital as a whole*.

Consider now, in the context of Okishio's theorem, the consequences of the generalisation of the new technique to all capitals in the sector, and the formation of new equilibrium prices and profit rate. It can be shown by mathematical techniques similar to those employed by Okishio that the short-term profit rate of the innovating capitalist is greater than the new long-term 'equilibrium' rate (after the diffusion of the technical change) which, in turn, is greater than the 'original' rate of profit (before the technical change). This implies that the capitalist who has acquired an advantage through technical innovation finds that this advantage is eroded as the innovation is generalised across the other capitals. The reduction of prices through the introduction of the new technique also reduces the rate of profit for the innovating capitalist. Therefore, for Okishio, price formation out of technical change acts for the *individual* innovating capitalist as a pressure reducing the rate of profit towards the (new) average. In contrast, for Marx, the process of price (and VCC) formation out of technical change is a counteracting tendency to the falling profitability for capital as a whole, since it leads to a reduction in the value of constant and variable capital that *results* from technical change.

Now put the two processes together, of introducing new technology and of generalising it across other producers to form new prices. For Okishio, these processes are immediate empirical phenomena. They do not interact with one another to give more complex and concrete outcomes; they are simply added together algebraically to form a sum of effects that leads to a rise in profitability for the economy as a whole. Moreover, the two disequilibrium processes cancel each other out and leave the system in harmonious equilibrium. Because of this, in the context of comparative statics, those who follow the Okishio approach never distinguish between the VCC and the OCC. Instead, they rely exclusively upon an equilibrium notion of the VCC which, nevertheless, is given the name organic composition. By contrast, for Marx, the law and the CTs are abstract tendencies whose interaction is not some simple algebraic sum but a crisis-ridden path of accumulation.

In spite of its limited scope, Okishio's result is powerful only in the sense that the rate of profit can empirically fall if wages rise. However, first, the rate of profit can fall for other reasons, unrelated to the level of wages, for example, if the economy suffers an adverse external shock (e.g. a deterioration in terms of trade due to higher imports prices). Second, and more importantly, Okishio's result is not necessary, because the outcome depends on the structures of production and demand, the impact of simultaneous changes in labour productivity, their effect on international competitivity, and so on. Specifically, even though higher wages could precipitate a crisis, capital accumulation can also *prosper* with rising real wages, because they lead to higher levels of consumption. In contrast, if real wages remain the same in spite of technical progress there is a reduction in the value of labour power and an increase in the rate of surplus value. These are CTs for Marx. That they exist, as a result of accumulation, does not guarantee the absence of crisis. Whereas these outcomes are always possible in the context of Marx's analysis of the LTRPF and the CTs, they are precluded by Okishio's narrow interest in the profit–wage ratio.

Issues and Further Reading

Issues around the LTRPF have been covered in the text. Karl Marx develops his analysis in Marx (1981a, part 3). The exposition in this book draws upon Ben Fine (1982, ch. 8 and, especially, 1992a) and Ben Fine and Laurence Harris (1979, ch. 4). For similar interpretations, see Duncan Foley (1986, ch. 8), Geert Reuten (1997), Roman Rosdolsky (1977, ch. 26) and John Weeks (1982a). Nobuo Okishio's (1961) critique of Marx has attracted enormous attention, most recently in *Research in Political Economy* (vol. 18, 2000), but see also Okishio's (2000) acknowledgement of the limitations in his original paper (including proposed changes that fail to address the problems identified in this chapter).

10
The Transformation Problem

In Volume 1 of *Capital* Marx is concerned with the production of value and surplus value and, in Volume 2, with its circulation and exchange. A major part of Volume 3 deals with distributional relations as they arise out of the interaction of production with exchange. In his analysis, Marx focuses on the distribution of the surplus value produced across the economy between competing industrial capitals, and between industrial capital as a whole, other forms of capital, including commercial and financial capital, and the landowning class.

Marx argues that industrial capitalists generally produce different quantities of surplus value with the same investment, because each capital employs a different quantity of value-producing labour. In spite of this, all capitals must (tendentially) enjoy equal rates of return, otherwise they would shift to more profitable areas of the economy. Marx explains the distribution of capital and labour across the economy, and the distribution of the surplus value produced by industrial capital (in the absence of other forms of capital), through the transformation of values into prices of production. At a more concrete level of analysis, commercial and financial capitalists, and the landowners, capture in exchange part of the surplus value produced by industrial capital. Marx explains these processes through his analysis of commercial profit, interest and rent (covered here, respectively, in chapters 11, 12 and 13).

From Values to Prices of Production

For the distribution of surplus value between capitalists in different sectors of the economy, Marx focuses initially on the tendency for the rate of profit to be equalised. Forming a general rate of profit by $r = S/(C + V)$, where the value quantities S, C and V are aggregates of surplus value and constant and variable capital for the economy as a whole, Marx argues that each capitalist would share in the surplus value produced according to their share in capital advanced. It is as if each capitalist receives a dividend on an equity share in the economy as a whole. As a result, the profit share of the *i*th capitalist, whose advance of constant and variable capital is $c_i + v_i$, would be represented by $r(c_i + v_i)$. For example, if the general profit rate is 50 per cent and the average capitalist, producing widgets, advances £100,000 (made up of variable and constant capital, including the depreciation of fixed capital), the firm's annual profits would (tendentially) be £50,000.

Corresponding to this would be a *price of production* for the commodity concerned, formed out of cost plus profit:

$$p_i = c_i + v_i + r(c_i + v_i) = (c_i + v_i)(1 + r)$$

A simple example will illustrate (see table 10.1).

Table 10.1 Marx's transformation*

Capitals ($M = c + v$)	Rate of surplus value ($e = s/v$)	Surplus value ($s = ev$)	Output value ($M' = c + v + s$)	'Value' rate of profit ($r = s/(c + v)$)	Price ($p = (c + v)(1 + r)$)	Profit ($\pi = p - (c + v)$)	'Price' rate of profit ($r = \pi/(c + v)$)
$60c + 40v$	1	40	140	0.4	150	50	0.5
$40c + 60v$	1	60	160	0.6	150	50	0.5
$100c + 100v$	1 (or 100%)	100	300	0.5 (or 50%)	300	100	0.5 (or 50%)

(*): The last row indicates totals or averages, where appropriate.

Suppose there are only two capitals producing distinct goods, one of which uses $60c + 40v$ and the other $40c + 60v$, with the rate of surplus value being 100 per cent. In this case, the value of the output of the first capital will be $60c + 40v + 40s = 140$, and the value of the output of the second capital will be $40c + 60v + 60s = 160$.

This example raises a serious problem. For it implies that, if capitalists advance equal sums of money but use distinct proportions of c and v, their profit rates are *different*. In our example, the first capital reaps only $r_1 = 40/(60 + 40) = 40$ per cent, while the second capital enjoys a much higher profit rate, $r_2 = 60/(40 + 60) = 60$ per cent. This is due to the difference in the composition of the advanced capitals, with a relatively higher proportion of variable capital leading to a higher profit rate. This should not be surprising. If only labour creates value (and, therefore, profit), while the means of production only transfer their value to the output, the capital employing more labour produces more value and surplus value and, all else constant, has a higher profit rate.

Capitals earning such different profit rates in different sectors will not co-exist for long, given the possibility of migration of capital across sectors. In other words, since each capitalist contributes equally in capital advanced (100), each must share equally in profit distributed (50 each). This can only come about if the prices of production are each 150. This is despite the differences in the values produced in the two sectors – in other words, the equalisation of profit rates between capitals operating in different sectors requires the *transfer* of (surplus) value across sectors of the economy.

In sum, since capitals in different sectors will generally use distinct quantities of labour, raw materials and machinery to produce commodities, Marx draws the conclusion that outputs do not exchange at their values but at prices of production. These prices of production differ from values, as the composition of capital, c_i/v_i, is greater or less than the average for the economy as a whole. (Note that for the first capital in table 10.1, $c_1/v_1 = {}^3/_2$ and, for the second, $c_2/v_2 = {}^2/_3$, compared with an average of 1 for the economy as a whole.)

Marx's Transformation and Its Critics

Marx's explanation of the relationship between values and prices has been, perhaps surprisingly, one of the most controversial aspects of his value theory. It has led some, even if otherwise sympathetic to Marxism, to reject the labour theory of value as irrelevant or even erroneous.

The reason for this reaction is that Marx's solution to the transformation problem is perceived to be incorrect, and that the consequences of this presumed 'error' are, supposedly, far-reaching. The crux of the critique is the following: Marx has shown that, when capitals compete across sectors (and migration of capital occurs), commodities no longer exchange at prices equal to their values. However, in doing so, he has continued to evaluate the inputs, c and v (and the 'value' rate of profit, used in the calculation of the prices of production) as if they were values, rather than prices. In other words, it is as if, for the critics, Marx presumes that commodities are purchased 'at values' as outputs (respectively, 140 and 160) but are sold 'at prices' as inputs (150 and 150), which is inconsistent as selling and buying prices must be the same.

For the problem of translating given values into prices of production in an economy in equilibrium, this is indeed a serious deficiency, but one of which Marx was fully aware and which can be corrected easily. It is merely a matter of transforming the inputs as well as the outputs, a simple algebraic procedure that does not need to be reproduced here. The implication of this 'correction' is straightforward: it shows that commodities have values as well as prices, and that two distinct accounting systems (not necessarily equally significant either in theory or in practice) are possible. One of these accounting systems expresses the socially necessary labour time required to produce each commodity, and the other the quantity of money which, in general, the commodity would fetch on sale.

More significant than this (or any other) algebraic solution of the 'transformation problem' is the observation that Marx's labour theory of value cannot founder on such quantitative conundrums, as the corrected algebraic solution seeks to imply. Crucially, Marx has shown that values exist as a consequence of the social relations between producers, and that price formation is a translation of production into exchange relations. Because they *exist* (rather than being merely a construct of the imagination), values cannot be rejected according to whether algebraic solutions to price theory are considered satisfactory or not. Rather, the *real* relationship between values and prices has to be recognised theoretically and explored analytically – for example, why do the dominant relations of production give rise to the value form, and how do values appear as prices in practice, and change over time.

In this light, it is significant to note that the transformation problem as traditionally conceived focuses on the implications of differences in the *value composition of capital* (VCC) across different sectors in the economy – as if *c* and *v* were quantities of *money* in table 10.1, with 140 and 160 being the 'original' prices of the unit of output, and 150 the unit prices 'modified by competition'.

This is *not* the case for Marx. For, in Volume 3, Marx considers the transformation entirely in terms of the *organic composition of capital* (OCC) which, as has already been shown in chapter 8, is only concerned with the effects of the differing rates at which raw materials are transformed into outputs (rather than with the differing values of the inputs themselves, which are captured by the VCC). As such, Marx is less concerned with how the inputs (*c* and *v*) have previously obtained their prices, and more concerned with how differing organic compositions affect the process of price and profit formation.

In other words, Marx's problem is the following. If a given amount of living labour in one sector (employed through the advance of variable capital *v*) works up a greater *quantity* of raw materials, represented by *c* (regardless of its cost) than in another sector, the commodities produced will command a higher price relative to value, as previously discussed and numerically illustrated in table 10.1. By the same token, the use of a greater *quantity* of labour in production will create more value and more profits than a lesser quantity – regardless of the sector, the use value being produced, and the cost of the raw materials. The use of the OCC, rather than the VCC, in Marx's analysis of the transformation is significant, because the OCC connects the rate of profit with the sphere of *production*, where living labour produces value and surplus value. In contrast, the VCC links the profit rate with the sphere of *exchange*, where commodities are traded and where the newly established values measure the rate of capital accumulation.

His emphasis on the OCC shows that Marx is primarily concerned with the effect on prices of the different (surplus) value-creating capacity of the advanced capitals, or the impact on prices of the different *quantities* of labour necessary to transform the means of production into the output – regardless of the value of the means of production being used as raw materials. The use of the OCC in the analysis of profit creation and distribution is important because it pins the source of surplus value and profit firmly down to *unpaid labour*. This helps Marx to substantiate his claims that machines do not create value, that surplus value and profit are not due to unequal exchange, and that industrial profit, interest and rent are shares of the surplus value produced by the productive wage workers.

The argument in this chapter illustrates that, in his transformation, Marx is not dealing with equilibrium price theory as in mainstream economics (and in conventional interpretations of Marx's theory), but with the relationship between differences or changes in production and price formation. This acts in Volume 3 as a prelude to the treatment of the law of the tendency of the rate of profit to fall (although the order of presentation is reversed in this book). Finally, the transformation problem and the LTRPF have generally been considered as two separate problems (although an author's stance on each has often been read as a commitment for or against Marx's value theory). However, in this chapter and the previous, through the consistent use of the OCC as distinguished from the VCC, it has been found that the two problems are closely related to each other. They are both concerned with the tensions created by the integration of production with exchange and, especially, with the consequences of differences or changes in conditions of production for price formation in particular, and movements in exchange more generally.

Issues and Further Reading

Again, issues concerning the transformation problem have been outlined in the text. It is remarkable how, even among those sympathetic to Marx, the problem has floated free from other 'problems' in Marx's political economy to become a debate over price formation in and of itself. Not surprisingly, the literature on the transformation problem is vast. The original treatment is presented in Marx (1981a, parts 1–2). The interpretation of the transformation in this chapter was pioneered by Ben Fine (1983a), and it is explained and developed further by Alfredo Saad-Filho (1997b and 2002 ch. 7). Several alternative approaches are available; for an overview, see Simon Mohun (1995) and Alfredo Saad-Filho (2002, ch. 2). Sraffian analyses, rejecting value theory as irrelevant and/or erroneous, are concisely presented in Ian Steedman (1977) – for critiques, see the papers in Ben Fine (1986) and Bob Rowthorn (1980), as well as Anwar Shaikh (1981 and 1982). Gérard Duménil (1980) and Duncan Foley (1982) have proposed a 'new interpretation' of the problem, focusing on the value of money as a means of resolving Marx's supposed conundrums. This is critically reviewed by Ben Fine, Costas Lapavitsas and Alfredo Saad-Filho (2004) and Alfredo Saad-Filho (1996).

11
Merchant's Capital

This chapter and the following outline Marx's theory of capital within the sphere of exchange. In earlier chapters, the focus has primarily been on the role of capital in producing surplus value, with exchange as a necessary but hardly explored complement. However, the analysis of profits and interest requires close study of capitalist activity other than in production, but in close relationship with the earlier topics of study. This chapter explains the category of merchant's capital. Chapter 12 investigates interest-bearing capital.

Marx's Category of Merchant's Capital

One of the themes running through Marx's treatment of capital in exchange is that there is a crucial distinction to be made between *money as money* and *money as capital* (see chapters 4 and 12). Money functions as money when it acts simply as a means of exchange between two agents, hence mediating commodity exchange, irrespective of the position of those agents in the circulation of capital as a whole – whether they be capitalists engaging in production or capitalists and workers engaging in consumption. Hence, the role of money as money is understood by reference to simple commodity circulation, $C - M - C$. By contrast, money as capital is understood by reference to the circuit of capital, $M - C \dots P \dots C' - M'$, where money is employed for the specific purpose of producing surplus value.

There is a definite relation between the two functions of money in capitalism, since the exchanges of simple commodity circulation and of industrial production are ultimately connected, most notably when we recognise that $C - M$ for one agent is $M - C$ for another. Further, both the use of money as money and as capital can involve credit relations as money is lent and borrowed to facilitate the acts of exchange involved. Marx analyses in detail the operation of money as money as part of merchant's capital.

Marx's treatment of merchant's capital is an abstract one. Although capitalist production and trade are closely intermingled, they are distinct and Marx identifies a tendency for the separation of these activities. This tendency must be reproduced in theory in order to comprehend the specific nature of merchant's capital, which is directed towards the carrying out of exchange alone.

Apart from the division between industrial capital, which produces surplus value, and merchant's capital, which circulates it and facilitates the transition between the commodity and money forms of capital (indirectly increasing the efficiency of industrial capital and, therefore, the mass of surplus value produced), Marx points out that merchant's capital itself tends to be divided into two forms: commercial capital (buying and selling of commodities) and money-dealing capital, or MDC (the handling of money).

With the development of capitalist production, the acts of buying and selling become the specialised tasks of particular capitalists (for example, transport, storage, retailing and wholesale), thereby creating a division of 'labour' among capitalists. In this case, industrial capitalists rely upon specialised merchant capitalists to undertake the realisation of (surplus) value. Furthermore, certain functions arising from the commodity form of production become the specialised activity of money dealers. These include book-keeping, the calculation and safeguarding of a money reserve, and the roles of cashiers and accountants.

Marx adds that merchant's capital is subject to mobility with industrial capital (industrial capitalists can move into trading, and vice versa) and, consequently, there is a tendency for the rate of return on merchant's capital to be equalised to the rate of profit on industrial capital, even though the former does not itself produce surplus value (which can only be created by productive labour engaged by industrial capital, see chapter 3).

Modified Prices of Production

The intervention of merchant's capital modifies the formation of prices of production, since capital advanced in the buying and selling of commodities does not produce surplus value, but tends to share equally in the surplus value distributed as profits. From the point of view of the commercial capitalists, the labour power purchased by them seems to be productive, because it is bought with variable capital with the intention of valorising the capital advanced. However, what it creates in fact is not surplus value, but merely the ability of the commercial capitalists to appropriate part of the surplus value produced by industrial capital. Therefore, the merchant costs (and profits on them) are not an addition to value, and commercial capital does not determine the price at which commodities are sold. Commercial profits are made up by merchants buying commodities *below* their prices of production, and selling them at their prices of production (examined in chapter 10).

Suppose, initially, that trading is costless and that merchants simply advance money of an amount B to perform their functions. Using the usual notation, the total capital advanced is now $C + V + B$, and the general rate of profit $r = S/(C + V + B)$. The industrialists sell commodities to merchants at prices below values, at an aggregate price $(C + V)(1 + r)$. In turn, the merchants add their profits to form the total selling price, $(C + V)(1 + r) + Br = C + V + (C + V + B)r$. But $(C + V + B)r = S$, so that the total selling price equals $C + V + S$, which is the total value produced.

The situation is slightly more complex when the merchants have costs other than the simple advance of money. These costs might include means of production used in the process of circulation and variable capital advanced as commercial wages. Let these costs be K_m. Following the above procedure, industrialists sell to merchants below value, at $(C + V)(1 + r)$. The merchants earn the average profit rate on their money advances B, as before, and recover their costs K_m together with profit on them. Since total value is equal to the total selling price, $C + V + S = (C + V)(1 + r) + Br + K_m(1 + r)$. This yields $r = (S - K_m)/(C + V + B + K_m)$. Not surprisingly, the additional capital advances K_m are reflected in the denominator; moreover, as costs, they also appear in the numerator as a deduction from surplus value to be distributed to capitalists as a whole.

Merchant's Capital at a More Complex Level

The theoretical distinction between industrial and merchant's capital is simple enough in principle, once we accept the corresponding distinction between the spheres of production and exchange in the circuit of industrial capital. But matters are not so simple in practice. For, historically and continuing to the present day, there are what might be termed 'hybrids' cutting across these distinctions. Some industrialists might undertake sales on their own account rather than relying upon specialised merchants serving the trade as a whole. Some merchants might also play a hand in organising production as in the putting out system or, more recently, the way in which clothing retailers draw upon a host of more or less sweated labour. Are these industrial or merchant's capital, or neither or both?

More generally, we often find that industrialists engage in different types of production, commerce and financial management. These overflows across boundaries do not deny the analytical distinction between production and exchange. However, they indicate that classification problems often cannot be resolved in theory, but only through detailed empirical investigation. Allocation of specific units of capital to one or another of the categories identified above depends essentially on the extent to which it is normal for these activities to be undertaken independently within the spheres of production or exchange (thereby setting standards for 'hybrids'). Also, as already hinted, since the division and allocation of industrial and merchant activity is subject to change, it is important to assess the dynamics of the relationship between the two and whether specific forms are transitional to more stable arrangements.

Perhaps an analogy will help. Take the self-employed. What is their status? They do not appear to be exploited wage workers. But what if their earnings are equivalent to those of a skilled wage earner, and they work just as long hours, and, possibly, for the same company? Then, effectively, the self-employed are wage workers in disguise. But what if earnings exceed value produced (e.g. top accountants and lawyers)? This example indicates that classification problems or the presence of hybrid categories need not invalidate abstract analysis. Indeed, it makes it even more essential if there is not to be a descent into ever more refined descriptive categories. However, the limits to abstract analysis must be acknowledged, and reference made to empirical realities, in order to proceed further.

The presence of these ambiguities, and the continuing dynamic or structural reasons for their existence, can only be identified empirically. Exactly the same applies to the distinctions between the spheres of production and exchange, and between industrial and merchant's capital. These points have been belaboured at some length here not only to unravel the conundrums around merchant's capital but also because they are of significance for the even more complex case of money and interest-bearing capital.

Issues and Further Reading

The Marxist literature on merchant's capital is limited and controversy has centred on whether merchant activity is productive or not (see chapter 3). Karl Marx's theory is developed in Marx (1981a, part 4). The interpretation in this chapter draws upon Ben Fine (1988) and Ben Fine and Ellen Leopold (1993, especially ch. 20); see also Duncan Foley (1986, ch. 7).

12
Banking Capital and the Theory of Interest

Marx's analysis of merchant's capital, explained in the previous chapter, is predicated upon the role of money as *money*. In contrast, his theory of interest-bearing capital (IBC) is based on the role of money as *capital*. This theory concerns the borrowing and lending taking place between, on the one hand, the money capitalists and, on the other hand, industrial or merchant capitalists. For Marx, it is not the act of borrowing from a bank or the payment of interest that characterises IBC, but the use to which the loan is put. The loan must be advanced as money capital and used to embark on a circuit of industrial capital. Therefore, to be able to use IBC is to be able to be a capitalist rather than simply to be able to borrow.

As the subject of borrowing and lending in this relationship, money capital becomes a special type of commodity. It provides the use value of self-expansion both for lender and borrower simultaneously, the former realising the interest and the latter the profit of enterprise that remains, after the payment of interest, from the surplus value produced through the use of the borrowed money capital. Marx emphasises that the price of this unique commodity (the interest rate) is 'irrational', since it bears no relation to any underlying production conditions. It depends upon the competitive relations governing the classes of borrowers and lenders. These issues are explored below.

Interest-Bearing Capital

Two characteristics distinguish IBC from industrial and merchant's capital. The first concerns the use of borrowing and lending (i.e. credit relations) specifically for the purpose of advancing money capital for the appropriation of surplus value. These credit relations involve the two most important fractions of the capitalist class: the money capitalists, who control the supply of IBC, and the industrial capitalists, who borrow IBC to use as capital in production and are responsible for the functioning of capital over the industrial circuit, supervising production and sale. To this division of the capitalist class corresponds a division of the surplus value extracted by the latter. As explained above, whereas the money capitalists receive interest, the industrial capitalists appropriate the profit of enterprise left over after the payment of interest (the determination of the rate of interest is discussed below).

Second, for its existence IBC draws upon the money capital accumulated through the sale of commodity capital, as well as the hoards of temporarily idle money of the industrial and commercial capitalists, workers, the state or anyone else. These hoards and savings are collected and centralised in the financial institutions, and transformed into potential money capital available to industrial capital. IBC therefore performs the ownership and control functions of money capital on behalf of capital as a whole. IBC is not, however, the juridical property of these institutions, and depositors are entitled to retrieve their funds (however, different types of financial investment may impose temporary restrictions on their ability to make withdrawals). Banks may also extend credit over and above their levels of deposits, and such credit can be used to initiate a circuit of industrial capital.

The differences between industrial capital and IBC are illustrated by their respective circuits. It was shown in chapter 4 that industrial capital is expressed by $M - C - M'$, for which money intervenes in the processes of production and exchange. In contrast, IBC is represented by $M - M'$, where money stands apart from these processes.

It is a constant theme throughout the three volumes of *Capital* that access to IBC holds the key to rapid accumulation. Increase in the size of capital, often achieved through borrowing, is one of the most important means of competitive accumulation. For example, the process of centralisation is generally financed by bank loans, and the size of capital plays a critical role in the pursuit of productivity increases through the introduction of more advanced machinery. It is through the detailed analysis of these relations and processes that Marx explains the structure of the financial system and its relationship with industrial capital.

Money Capital and the Financial System

Marx's distinction between industrial capital and IBC does not always translate neatly into empirical analysis, as exemplified in the previous chapter for the 'hybrids' attached to merchant's capital. This is so for two main reasons.

On the one hand, the functions of money as money can be undertaken by various financial instruments – a credit card, for example, can serve as means of payment but it cannot settle all accounts once and for all. As a result, there is a complex and overlapping cascade of monetary instruments, with 'money proper' at its pinnacle, serving across all functions and circumstances – whether it be the US dollar or something else that is as good as gold. By the same token, the activities associated with money-dealing capital (MDC), such as book-keeping, the calculation and safeguarding of a money reserve and the role of cashier, can be performed in different ways, for example, in-house (when firms hire their own accountants or create specialised divisions to speculate over exchange rate movements and in futures and options markets), by specialist firms outside the banking system, or by financial institutions. In analytical terms, even if these activities are performed in-house by industrial capital (as was often the case at earlier stages of capitalist development or, today, for small firms), they are a function of merchant's capital and attract the normal rate of profit even though they do not produce surplus value (see chapter 11). Whatever the circumstances, three analytical distinctions separate MDC from IBC: MDC advances credit in general, whereas IBC uses credit relations to advance money capital in order to appropriate surplus value; MDC captures part of industrial profit (in the same way as commercial capital), whereas IBC leads to the division of surplus value into interest and profit of enterprise; and, finally, the return on MDC is limited by the general profit rate while the rate of return on IBC exceeds the normal rate of profit (see below). In spite of these differences, in contemporary society, in which MDC has reached a high level of development, the functions of MDC are normally undertaken by the banking system, and the resources involved become part of IBC. The upshot is that it can be very difficult in practice to classify firms and the resources they control to one or the other category of industrial, money-dealing or interest-bearing capital, and there is considerable scope for the existence of 'hybrids' in practice.

On the other hand, IBC can be party to various operations targeted at producing or appropriating surplus value, either independently or in association with industrial capital. The credit system extends the limits of the reproduction process and accelerates the development of the productive forces and the world market. The returns on these operations may vary according to the fortunes of the capitalist economy and specific investments, as with shares or venture capital, or these returns may be designated in advance or be (considered) more or less risky. Whatever the form and conditions taken by these transactions, IBC attaches itself through them to the circulation and economic reproduction of capital as a whole. Through these relationships IBC represents a claim on surplus value that has yet to be produced, whether it be through transactions involving payments that have yet to be made, or the transformation of these claims into tradable assets, ranging over bully-boy debt collectors to government bonds, as well as foreign exchange markets, futures markets for commodities that have yet to be produced, and so on. In turn, these markets breed upon one another, with financial services being sold as portfolios of assets, as in pension funds and investment trusts. Each of these is a paper claim to property that may or may not include productive capital that may or may not generate or appropriate surplus value, what Marx terms 'fictitious capital'.

In this light, it is hardly surprising that the financial sector should be capable of financing overproduction and generating spectacular speculative bubbles and equally spectacular crashes. Nor is it surprising that the possibility of fraud is ever present. The division between finance and industry and the shifting balance between them are dramatically illustrated by the developments in world finance and national financial systems over the past 30 years. The bloated and heavily rewarded international financial system has benefited at the expense of real accumulation and, over the past decade, has been subject to severe crises. In Volume 3 of *Capital* Marx investigates the circumstances in which the accumulation of IBC and the assets and markets built upon it can be validated by the accumulation of real capital. He concludes that no answer can be given in advance, because there can be no guarantee of production and appropriation of surplus value (see chapter 7). For example, the owner of IBC might advance to an industrialist who is corrupt, incompetent or thwarted, or to a consumer who is unable or refuses to pay back. In either case, the circuit of IBC can be interrupted with potentially severe implications for the reproduction of both interest-bearing and industrial capital.

In conclusion, the division between industrial capital and IBC is the outcome of an intermingling of circuits of capital without predetermined outcomes in terms of real accumulation. For this basic reason, neither the functioning of the financial system nor its interaction with real accumulation can be subject to control in the sense of, putting it in mainstream terms, fixing the supply of money or tying it (or its cost) to the level of real economic activity. This is not to suggest that private or public regulation of the financial system, including monetary policy, cannot have an effect on outcomes. But the idea that fictitious capital can be aligned to real accumulation through regulation is misguided, because fictitious capital has become increasingly necessary for real accumulation but cannot guarantee it. By the same token, the nature of the financial system and its interaction with real accumulation cannot be logically predetermined by abstract analysis. Rather, they evolve together over the longer term establishing particular structures of financial and industrial activity, as well as specific outcomes during the course of crises.

Interest as an Economic Category

Drawing upon the above analysis, it is possible to identify four distinguishing features of Marx's theory of interest. First, it starts with the structural separation between control of money capital and control of productive capital, as well as the socio-political balance of power between the money and industrial capitalists, rather than 'technical' or institutional factors or the supply and demand for money capital. These analytical factors must be contextualised within a broader social and historical theory rather than being deployed without regard for the different ways in which they are influential at each point in time. For Marx, the mode of integration between the two fractions of the capitalist class, and the division of surplus value between them, cannot be determined in the abstract. There is no 'natural' (or long-term equilibrium) rate of interest to be earned by the owners of IBC, and the actual levels and term structure of the market interest rate cannot be determined purely theoretically.

Second, the separation explained above is reflected in the structural differences between the competitive processes taking place within the industrial and IBC sectors. In the industrial sector, competition through capital mobility, stock market activity and access to IBC creates a tendency towards uniformity of rates of profit. However, this process is both slow and uneven because of the existence of numerous obstacles in the way of profit rate equalisation (see chapter 6). In contrast, competition within the IBC sector creates powerful tendencies towards both uniformity in rates of interest and, at a further remove, the equalisation of rates of return across the firms operating in this sector. These tendencies are realised much more rapidly than in the industrial sector, because of the extraordinary mobility of money within the IBC sector and the uniformity of the 'commodity' involved.

Third, although interest is a deduction of the surplus value extracted by industrial capital, the rate of return on IBC generally *exceeds* the normal rate of profit on industrial capital. For equality between them would require that competition within the fraction of IBC be as intense as competition between the sectors of industrial capital. But while competition between industrial capitals is, in part, fought by access to greater quantities of IBC, there are limitations on the extent to which this can occur within the banking sector itself. The potential sources of money capital for further accumulation in the IBC sector are not systematically available to all capitalists through the credit system, because the banks rarely make loans to finance potential rivals (including those intent on migrating from the industrial sector); rather, the banks would tend to use the available resources to increase their own profitability. Moreover, the unrestricted mobility between industrial capital and IBC would result in the ineffectiveness of IBC's control of society's idle money capital. In other words, whereas industrial capital cannot in general enter the IBC sector to compete with it, IBC can search out the highest return across all sectors including its own. Therefore, IBC tends to earn a rate of return over and above the normal rate of profit. Obviously, the extent of the profitability differences and their fluctuations over time cannot be determined in the abstract.

Fourth, the level of the interest rate is 'accidental', being determined by a range of institutional factors and the supply and demand for loanable money capital rather than the law of value (whether at the relatively abstract level of socially necessary labour times or the more concrete level of profit rate equalisation). These factors include the rhythm of industrial expansion, the balance of payments and the finances of the state, the structure of payments and financial services in the economy and the extent of financial speculation. In spite of this large degree of indeterminacy, the mass of interest is necessarily limited by the mass of profit.

Marx's ability to construct a distinct theory of interest as opposed to profit is a distinguishing mark of his economic analysis. In Classical political economy, for example, interest is a category introduced with little if any explanation, and the rate of interest oscillates around an arbitrary 'natural' rate for which there are no determinants other than supply of and demand for money. Equally, within neoclassical economics, most notably for the Fisherian theory of intertemporal consumption and production, the rates of interest and profit are conceptually identical, and quantitatively equal in equilibrium. Even for Keynesian economics (and for Keynes himself), where monetary factors are specifically introduced, the rate of profit – as represented by the marginal efficiency of capital – is set equal to the rate of interest. Moreover, while short-term expectations may lead to a disequilibrium value of the rate of interest, underlying Keynesianism is the idea that there is a full-employment natural or equilibrium interest rate. This significant divergence from Marx's theory is intimately connected to the failure of Keynesian theory to differentiate between demand, and hence credit, for accumulation and for consumption, except for multiplier purposes.

In contrast, Marx not only categorises interest distinctively, he also locates it within the analytical structure of his economic thought, deriving interest from the competitive relations between two clearly distinguished fractions of the capitalist class. He does so by reference to the abstract tendencies and structures that he has identified for the capitalist economy, e.g. for the rate of profit to be equalised, for the credit system to be the mechanism of competition in accumulation, for money to stand apart from other commodities, for idle hoards to be centralised in the banking system, and so on. These abstract considerations are brought to bear on the historical and empirical analysis of IBC and the financial structures of specific social formations, which must be discovered by empirical analysis. Marx had much to say on these issues, especially in his study of the British financial system in Volume 3 of *Capital*, but this complex material is not covered here.

Issues and Further Reading

In spite of their enormous importance for contemporary capitalism, Marxian studies of money and finance have progressed relatively slowly, with little generally being said about the more fundamental issues of the nature of finance and the relationship between financial and industrial capital (other than pointing out the increasing prominence of the former, especially in the historical epoch of neoliberalism).

Karl Marx's theory of IBC and interest is outlined in Marx (1981b and, especially, 1981a, part 5). This chapter draws upon Ben Fine (1985–86). Different aspects of Marx's theory of money and credit are explained by Suzanne de Brunhoff (1976 and 2003), Duncan Foley (1986, ch. 7), David Harvey (1999, chs 9–10), Rudolf Hilferding (1981), Makoto Itoh and Costas Lapavitsas (1999), Costas Lapavitsas (2000a, 2000b, 2003a, 2003b), Costas Lapavitsas and Alfredo Saad-Filho (2000), Roman Rosdolsky (1977, ch. 27) and John Weeks (1981, ch. 5).

13
Marx's Theory of Agricultural Rent

Marx's theory of rent contains two important and closely connected components, a theory of differential rent and a theory of absolute rent. The basis on which Marx analyses rent theory is one in which private ownership of land acts as a potential obstacle to capital accumulation in the agricultural sector, and captures part of the surplus value produced in the economy. To a limited extent the same is true of orthodox rent theory, whether neoclassical or Ricardian (although, importantly, whereas Ricardo attempted to distinguish analytically between rent and profit, neoclassical theory does precisely the opposite, as is shown below). In orthodox theory, the producers pay rent because of a combination of private ownership and natural or technical constraints – for example, a shortage of land, either in overall supply or in the supply of land of better quality or location. In more sophisticated accounts, the demand for the different products of land may also be taken into account. In either case, rent serves in part to allocate resources efficiently across different lands to serve consumption.

Two interesting properties follow from the orthodox view. First, ownership of land as such is irrelevant; it merely determines who is to receive the rent, not its level.

Second, the level of rent is determined by the technical conditions of production (and demand). These properties of the orthodoxy have been brought to the fore in order to highlight the major differences with Marx's approach. For Marx, the starting point is the conditions under which part of the surplus value is appropriated by the landowners in the form of rent. As such, rent theory depends on the specification of the relationship between landed property and capitalist production and these are, of necessity, historically specific and variable (rather than technically given). Consequently, there can be no general theory of rent, and the conclusions reached in one instance cannot automatically be applied to others.

In other words, rent cannot be analysed simply on the basis of a general effect, for example, of impeding capitalist production. Otherwise, 'rent' would be the outcome of any obstacle to capitalist investment (which is the gist of the Marshallian notion of quasi-rents in the short run, when one capitalist temporarily profits from a superior method of production). In this case, privileged access to finance or markets and a host of other conditions would have to be treated on a par with rent theory (as can be seen in the neoclassical theory of 'rent-seeking'), and a specific theory of the social role of landed property would be lost. In short, rent must be examined in conjunction with specific historical conditions, particularly as capitalism, as a mode of production, tends to sweep aside the barriers to its imperative to accumulate. Why and how does landed property limit capital accumulation, and successfully extract a share of the surplus value pumped out by industrial capital?

This is the most demanding chapter in this book. It is included here for two reasons: first, because it illustrates in detail an important application of Marx's method, and confronts an issue that allegedly contradicts his value theory; and second, because of the continuing relevance of rent for issues as diverse as oil, mining, agricultural development and urban regeneration.

Differential Rent 1

Marx's theory of differential rent (DR) can be understood only by examining how landed property intervenes in the operation of capital within agriculture. How is it that the competitive process leaves surplus value to be appropriated in the form of rent, and what are the implications of this? To confront this problem, a slight digression is needed to examine how capitals compete with each other within a sector in the absence of a significant distorting effect from land.

It was shown in chapters 6 and 8 that capitals within the same sector compete with each other primarily by raising productivity through increases in the organic composition of capital (OCC). This does not occur evenly across the sector, so there will tend to be significant productivity differences between these capitals. Marx argues that commodity values are formed out of these different individual productivities. Significantly, he does not insist that values must equal the average labour time for the sector (even assuming that the workers are identical across the economy). For example, if either the most favourable or the least favourable technique is sufficiently weighty as compared with the average, then the technique concerned rather than the average regulates the sector's market value. In either case, *excess* or *surplus profits* will accrue to those capitals whose productivity is higher than the sectoral average.

Marx's explanation of DR1 starts with the existence of surplus profits in agriculture because of fertility differences (ignoring transport and other costs). This is usually associated with Ricardo's extensive margin. In brief, capital cannot flow evenly onto lands of equal fertility, since they are not necessarily available. Those capitals that do flow onto the better lands meet the barrier of landed property, and are forced by the landowners to forgo more or less of their surplus profit in the form of rent. The result is not simply the creation of rent, but also a distortion in the formation of market value in agriculture. In industry, the worst methods of production predominate only where they are exceptionally weighty, and capitals employing more productive methods capture surplus profits. In contrast, in agriculture the worst methods can predominate because of the intervention of landed property, and the capitals invested in better (non-marginal) lands may be required to surrender their surplus profits in the form of DR1 to landowners. For Ricardo, these possible roles for landed property must prevail irrespective of ownership of land (which, for him, merely determines who receives the fertility-determined rents). By contrast, for Marx, rent always depends upon the effective presence of landed property, and its capacity to appropriate the differential surplus attached to lands of different quality.

Thus, the existence of profitability differences within the agricultural sector is a necessary but insufficient condition for the existence of DR1. These surplus profits must also be permanent and appropriated by sufficiently powerful landlords, otherwise (as in Marshall's quasi-rents) DR1 would not only exist in every sector of the economy, but it would also be eroded like the surplus profits (which tend to be competed away because of capital movements and the diffusion of technological innovations within each sector). However, it should be noted that differing natural conditions as such are not the source of DR1. They may contribute to productivity differences, but they do not create either the categories of surplus profit or differential rent. For DR depends upon the utilisation of natural conditions (and productivity differences) under capitalist relations of production, as well as the intervention of landed property. In other words, rent exists not because surplus profits exist, but because they are appropriated by the landowner rather than by the capitalist.

Differential Rent 2

Marx's theory of DR1 is constructed on the basis of *equal* applications of capital to *different* lands, in which case surplus profits (and rent) arise from the more or less permanent fertility differences across these lands. Differential rent of the second type (DR2) is also concerned with competition within the agricultural sector. However, DR2 is due to the appropriation of the surplus profits created by temporary productivity differences arising from the application of *unequal* capitals to *equal* lands. In this case, the landowners benefit from the progress of society in introducing technical innovations and organising large-scale production on individual lands, so the owners of those lands may appropriate a share of the added surplus.

As accumulation in agriculture proceeds, raising productivity and surplus, landed property may appropriate an increased share of the surplus.

Clearly, though, the entire surplus profits that form the potential basis of DR2 may not accrue to the landowners, and these surplus profits tend to be eroded as the abnormal size of the capital investments becomes normal across the sector. However, DR2 necessarily reduces the incentive to capitalist farmers to invest intensively (more capital and better technology on the same land) rather than extensively (same technology across more land), which blunts the technological development of agriculture. This is why Marx argues that, whilst agriculture may not resist absolutely the capitalist form of development, it tends to exhibit a slow pace of progress relative to industry. This is perhaps the most important conclusion to be drawn from Marx's theory of DR2: its dynamic preoccupation with obstacles to the development of capital accumulation, rather than the static formulation of the distribution of surplus value in the form of rent.

If DR1 and DR2 were independent of each other, the analysis of DR, as the simple addition of DR1 and DR2, would now be complete. For then DR1 would have the effect of equalising lands so that DR2 could be calculated from the profitability of unequal capitals. Alternatively, DR2 would equalise the effects of different applications of capital so that DR1 could be calculated from the differing fertilities between lands. This procedure is, however, invalid. In fact, in Volume 3 of *Capital* Marx never examines DR2 in the pure form of unequal applications of capital to equal lands. He always discusses DR2 in the presence of DR1 – that is, of lands of unequal quality.

Marx's reason for doing so is to analyse the quantitative determination of DR2 having laid down the qualitative basis for its existence.

In this chapter, DR1 and DR2 have each been determined on the basis of certain abstractions concerning the distribution of capitals and fertilities. This has been done for expositional clarity, but there is no presumption that the interaction of DR1 and DR2 is simply additive. A more complex analysis is necessarily involved concerning the co-existence of unequal lands and unequal capitals on those lands. For DR1, there is the problem of determining the worst land in the presence of unequal applications of capital (DR2). For example, some lands may be worse for one level of investment but not for others. For DR2, there is the problem of determining the normal level of investment in the presence of differing lands (DR1). Some capitals may be normal for some types of lands, other capitals normal for other lands. There is a further difficulty for DR2, since the decreasing productivity of additional investments would not allow for surplus profits for abnormally large capitals unless the market value of the agricultural product rises. This raises the question of whether the market value should be determined by the individual productivity of some plot of land, or whether it may be determined by some part of the capital invested in that land. In other words, is the size of 'normal capital' always the total capital applied to some land, or can it be some part of that capital? Even the term normal capital can be inappropriate, for capital investment in a particular land is always specific rather than general.

These problems concern the simultaneous determination of *worst land* and *normal capital* in agriculture. The interaction of the two gives rise to the market value of agricultural produce, from which differential rents can be calculated. This problem does not arise for industrial capital, because the determination of normal capital is synonymous with the determination of value. It was shown above that the same is true for each of DR1 and DR2 in the absence of the other. For DR1 in its pure form (equal capitals) the determination of worst land is synonymous with the determination of value, whereas for DR2 in its pure form (equal lands) it is the determination of normal capital that comes to the fore in the determination of value.

This problem of the joint determination of normal capital and worst land (or, more exactly, normal land, since the physically worst land in use may not be the one to determine value) cannot be resolved abstractly; correspondingly, DR1 and DR2 cannot be determined purely theoretically. As discussed previously, they depend upon historically contingent conditions, on how agriculture has developed in the past and how it relates to capital accumulation in terms of capitalists' access to the land (which may be affected by legal, financial and other conditions). Moreover, changes in crops and production technologies modify the demand for land, and the definitions of best and worst land. In short, DR theory does not specifically lead to a determinate analysis of rent, but reveals the processes by which it may be examined historically.

Absolute Rent

If the key to the formation of differential rent is the determination of value and the presence of surplus profits in the agricultural sector, the basis for the formation of absolute rent (AR) is the transformation from market values into prices of production (see chapter 10). In this sense, AR departs from DR. Both forms of rent concern the obstacle to capital investment posed by landed property, and the appropriation of surplus profit in the form of rent. However, DR and AR are located at different levels of analysis and, therefore, their source is correspondingly different. DR derives from productivity differences within agriculture, while AR derives from the productivity differences between agriculture and other sectors of the economy.

In purely formal terms, Marx's theory of AR is as follows: because of the barriers imposed by landed property, explained in the analysis of DR2, agriculture tends to have a lower OCC than industry; therefore, there is a higher proportion of living labour employed in agriculture, this sector produces additional surplus value and, in the absence of rent, its price of production would be below value.

This is, however, an entirely static account. In dynamic terms, with algebraic details taken up below, the formation of prices of production depends upon competition and the possibility of capital flows between sectors. However, flows into agriculture, and the formation of prices of production in this sector, are obstructed by landed property. Because of this obstacle, landowners can charge an AR for capital flows on to new land (or DR2 for flows into existing lands in use). This charge increases the price of agricultural commodities above their price of production. In the limit, these commodities might be sold at value, with the difference between their sale price and price of production being captured as AR. Under these circumstances, the conditions in which AR would disappear are (a) if the pace of development of agriculture were equal to that of industry, and agriculture's OCC were equal to (or higher than) the social average, and (b) if all land had been taken into cultivation, since AR depends upon capital movements on to new lands.

In the literature, one often finds another interpretation of Marx's theory of AR, in which the landowners capture a rent because they can prevent the flow of capital into agriculture. However, this is simply AR as a monopoly rent. Similar considerations would apply in the absence of landed property – for example, if there were an essential patent involved in the production process. This is insufficient for two reasons. First, because this theory is liable to be a static theory of surplus value distribution. Second, in this interpretation Marx's conditions for the existence of AR become purely arbitrary. This is true of the dependence of AR on low OCC in agriculture, particularly when it is recognised that OCCs differ between industrial sectors without rent being formed. Moreover, even in agriculture there would be no reason for AR to be limited to the difference between value and price of production. If AR were a monopoly rent, the market price of agricultural commodities could rise above their value according to the ability and willingness of the landowners to impose such high prices.

However, Marx's discussion of the conditions under which AR would disappear suggests that a static theory is not involved. What matters, as was explained above, is the pace of development of agriculture relative to industry and the movement of capital on to new lands. Of course, these conditions can be interpreted statically (for example, assuming that all land is leased and all sectors have equal levels of development) but, otherwise, the other concepts utilised, in particular the OCC, must be interpreted in the dynamic of Marx's theory of accumulation. In undertaking this task, it will be shown below that Marx's theory of AR is fully consistent with his analysis of capital.

Suppose initially that the OCC is given by c/v, and that it can be increased in any sector (including agriculture) by a factor $b > 1$, so that a given quantity of labour would convert bc constant capital into final goods, rather than c. For agriculture, the difference between value and price of production (d) is:

$$d = [c + v + s] - [(c + v)(1 + r)] = s - (c + v)r$$

where r is the rate of profit. With technical change, the rate of profit changes from $r = s/(c + v)$ to $s/(bc + v)$. Therefore, the difference between value and price of production becomes:

$$d = s - \frac{(c+v)s}{bc+v} = \frac{(bc+v)s-(c+v)s}{bc+v}$$

$$d = (b-1)cr$$

This difference is equal to the rate of profit multiplied by the additional constant capital set in motion or, alternatively, the surplus profits arising out of the higher OCC. These surplus profits would be captured as DR2 if the OCC increased on the lands currently in use. In sum, the AR is limited by the maximum charge for extensive cultivation into new lands, permitted by the possibility of competing investment in intensive cultivation. This corresponds to the difference between value and price of production in agriculture.

It has been shown above that Marx's theory of rent is a coherent extension of his theory of capital to accumulation confronting the barrier of landed property. For him, rent is the economic form of class relations in agriculture, and it can be understood only by examining the relationship between capital and land. Rent depends upon the production and appropriation of surplus value through the intervention of landed property. Differential rent depends upon the existence of surplus profits formed through competition within the agricultural sector. DR1 results from productivity differences due to 'natural' conditions, leading to equal capitals earning different profit rates in agriculture. DR2 results from the different returns of unequal applications of capital (capitals of different sizes) in agriculture. In industry, the surplus profits accrue to the most productive capital. In contrast, in agriculture they may be appropriated as rent. Finally, AR arises from the difference between value and price of production in agriculture, because of its lower than average OCC.

Marx's theory of rent draws upon his theories of production, accumulation, the formation of value and the theory of prices of production. As such, it is probably the most complex application of his understanding of the capitalist economy. At the same time, it clearly reveals its own limits in showing how further analysis is contingent upon exactly how landed property has developed and interacts with capitalist development.

Issues and Further Reading

Most controversial in Marx's theory of rent (more exactly, landed property) is whether and how he differs from Ricardo in the theory of differential rent, whether absolute rent is monopoly rent or not and whether lower OCC in agriculture is arbitrary (together with AR being limited to the difference between value and price). The importance of Marx's theory, however, lies less in providing a determinate theory of rent and price and more in drawing attention to the historically specific ways in which landed property influences the pace, rhythm and direction of capital accumulation – whether in the context of agriculture, oil or urban regeneration.

Marx's theory of rent is developed especially in Karl Marx (1969, chs 1–14 and 1981a, part 6). This chapter draws upon Ben Fine (1982, chs 4, 7, 1986 and 1990b). For similar approaches, see Cyrus Bina (1989), David Harvey (1999, ch. 11) and Isaak I. Rubin (1979, ch. 29).

14
Conclusion: Marxism and the Twenty-First Century

The popularity and prominence of Marxism rises and falls with intellectual fashions and with the rhythm of world events. These two influences are far from independent of one another and, further, what is understood to be the content and emphasis of Marxism is equally variable across time, place and context. It ranges from critique of capitalism, currently to the fore in the presumed era of globalisation, to providing alternatives to it, as with the (previously) socialist countries and the struggles to construct post-colonial alternatives to capitalism. Marxism has also been heavily embroiled in all the major academic debates across the social sciences although, once again, the weight and content of its presence have been both diverse and uneven over time, topic and discipline.

The purpose of this final chapter is to argue for the continuing salience of Marx's political economy for the study of contemporary issues. Necessarily, it can only be suggestive and limited in coverage. As the body of this book has covered political economy the focus, below, is shifted to 'non-economic' issues. An appropriate starting point is the major academic assault that was made against Marxism since its last peak of popularity during the 1960s and 1970s. Apart from the mythical idea that Keynesianism had more or less resolved the problem of capitalist crises, anti-Marxism flourished through suggesting that Marxism was crude and doctrinaire. Two intimately connected issues in particular came to the fore – one concerned the nature of class and the other the nature of the (capitalist) state. Concerns with the environment and the aftermath of capitalism are also examined below.

Class

The major criticism made against Marxism with respect to class is its supposed inability to deal with the complexity and diversity of class relations within advanced capitalist society, variously dubbed as post-industrial, democratic, welfarist, and so on. The critique has two separate components, one concerning class *structure*, the other concerning the *implications* of that structure. In short, and partly because Marx allegedly predicted increasing polarisation in class structure (including, wrongly, the 'absolute' pauperisation of the workers), it is argued that the division between bourgeoisie and proletariat is too crude and, not least because of Marx's revolutionary aspirations for the working class, class action and ideology have presumably failed to match his expectations and those corresponding to his posited class structure. For example, why do wage workers vote for right-wing governments and why do conservative governments introduce reforms that benefit working people? These questions are taken up below. At a methodological level, there are concerns over both the structure of Marx's theory and its causal content. For example, it is deemed to be too deterministic and reductionist – supposedly implying that everything flows from the economic, with the economic itself identified primarily with production and class relations.

No doubt many Marxists have been guilty of these analytical sins of oversimplification and omission of other factors, if in part in the attempt to expose the fallacies of 'freedom', 'efficiency' and 'equality' that are too readily paraded as virtues of capitalism. Hopefully, though, enough of Marx's political economy and method has already been presented in this book to show that Marx himself could not reasonably be accused of these shortcomings. Indeed, Marx once declared himself as not a Marxist in view of the way his method had been abused in his own lifetime!

More specifically, in the case of class, Marx's political economy reveals the crucial and core component of the class structure of capitalism – that capital and labour necessarily confront one another over the buying and selling of labour power. Further, as presented in this book, Marx's political economy is concerned with the consequences of this class structure for accumulation, reproduction, uneven development, crises, and so on. Thus, far from reducing all other economic and social phenomena to such analysis, Marx's political economy does no more (although it is a great deal and of crucial importance) than open the way for broader, systematic and more complex investigation of the structure, relations, processes and consequences of capitalism.

Thus, Marx's political economy does not reduce the class structure to that of capital and labour. On the contrary, other classes are located in relation to capital and labour whether as an essential or contingent part of the capitalist mode of production. Within capitalism itself, for example, scope is created for the self-employed to emerge and for 'professionals' to prosper because, for different reasons, they are able to retain the full fruits of their labour despite being paid a wage or, more exactly, a salary. Formally, this can be represented by the idea that such strata receive the full reward for their living labour, $l = v + s$, rather than remuneration at the value of labour power, v. More important, though, is to explain why such strata, and their associated activities and conditions of work, are not appropriated by capital.

A number of general arguments can be given, some structural and some contingent. Thus, for example, a precondition for advanced capitalism is the emergence of sophisticated credit and commercial systems in which handsome rewards accrue to those who actively mobilise and allocate funds and commodities on behalf of others. The same applies to the professions needed to oil or safeguard the circulation of capital in all its aspects, and its social reproduction more generally, although these vary in weight and significance across time and place and are subject to proletarianisation where professional associations prove ineffective. There are, after all, huge differences between the 'self-employed' casual building worker or contracted-out cleaner and the specialist doctor or management consultant.

Finally, what is perceived to be the greatest challenge to the political economy of class is the rise of the middle class, itself a highly diverse stratum in terms of its composition and characteristics. Advanced capitalism has witnessed the decline of the industrial worker and the rise of services, especially those employed by the state and, thereby, potentially removed from direct commercial motivation and calculation. In short, does the growing army of health, education and other workers employed by the state, quite apart from those in the private services sector, undermine analysis predicated upon a class structure composed of capital and labour?

Posing the issue in these terms points to the continuing relevance of economic class, with labour defined in terms of its dependence upon a wage. This is not to deny that the class of labour is heavily differentiated among itself, even in economic terms – by sector, skill (manual or mental), labour process, engaged in industry or commerce, and for the public or private sector. Such differentiation does not invalidate the concept of class. What it does do is to highlight that class interests and actions do not always, or even predominantly, exist as an immediate consequence of class structure. Rather, class interests are necessarily formed economically, politically and ideologically in ways that arise socially and historically out of the class relations from which they derive. Thus, it is not a matter of allocating one or other individual to this or that class on the basis of their individual characteristics – manual workers, trade unionists, members of workers' parties, or whatever – but of tracing out the relations by which the working class is reproduced and represented in material and ideological relations. On this basis, there can be no neat or fixed correspondence between economic and other social characteristics, but nor are these entirely independent of one another. That the working class (i.e. the wage earners, rather than the much narrower sub-set of blue-collar industrial workers) depends upon wages for its reproduction conditions every aspect of contemporary social life, even where it appears to be otherwise, but it does not subject them to iron determination in incidence and content.

These general observations on class have relevance for the theory of the capitalist state. Once again, Marxism has been subject to criticism in the form of parody, with its theory of the state perceived as reducing to the simple proposition that it serves the ruling class and, hence, capitalist interests. This is immediately open to the objection that the state often implements policies that benefit working people, especially through welfare reform. Crudely portrayed Marxism is then thought to defend itself through understanding reform as a devious strategy on the part of the ruling class to pre-empt revolution where it is not otherwise securing a working class better able to produce (and fight wars) on its behalf.

As before, the historical record fails to bear out such simple motives for the timing and content of reform, and nor is it sufficient to explain provision of health, education and welfare as simply the means by which to enhance short- or long-term labour productivity. Another popular misrepresentation of Marxist theory is to view the state as essential in mediating between conflicting interests *within* the capitalist class, rather than between capital and labour. In this case, the main function of the state is to prevent capitalists from cheating one another, and the intensity of competition from being unduly dysfunctional. Like the theory of the state as the instrument of one class against another, this approach only sheds limited light on the complexity and diversity of the state's role and actions.

The problem in each of these cases is that the state is seen as an internally homogeneous institution clearly separated from 'the market' and an instrument serving readily identifiable interests – of capital against labour, or for capital as a whole against the destructive inclinations of its individual elements, or even for 'the nation' against rival nations and capitals. But such interests do not and cannot always exist in such highly abstract, and yet easily recognisable, forms. Rather, classes and class interests are formed through economic, political and ideological actions, conditioned if not rigidly determined by the accumulation of capital and the patterns of social reproduction (including employment structures, conditions of work, trade union and other forms of activity and daily reproduction at home, in the workplace and elsewhere) upon which class formation depends to a greater or lesser extent and in diverse ways.

In each of these areas, the capitalist state occupies an increasingly central role. The circulation of capital carves out an economic sphere of activity that is structurally separate from the non-economic but, simultaneously, dependent upon and supporting it. Workers' compliant observance of property relations and legitimation of economic and other inequalities need to be reproduced at least as much as immediate value relations. Thus is structurally created the necessity of the capitalist state largely by virtue of its non-economic role. Even so, the state is always heavily and directly embroiled in the economic life of capitalism – appropriating and disbursing (surplus) value through taxation and expenditure, regulating accumulation, restructuring capital as it goes through its cyclical patterns, manipulating exchange rates through monetary and other macroeconomic policies, and influencing distributional relations through taxation and incomes policy.

Unfortunately, these critically important insights from Marxism have often been overlooked, even when Marx has been commended for his foresight in anticipating globalisation or for recognising similar processes on an earlier historical stage. Certainly Marx does emphasise the international character of capitalism, and its restless search for profits wherever they can be found. This forges affinities with those who understand globalisation in terms of the withering away of the nation-state as it becomes increasingly powerless against an increasingly internationally mobile capital that is perceived to roam as effortlessly as the transfer of finance through electronic trading.

However, whatever the level of internationalisation of capital in its three forms (of money, commodities and production), the non-economic reproduction of capitalism inevitably requires and even strengthens the role of the nation-state, although this does not lead to uniformity through pressure to conform to the one-dimensional imperatives of commerce. In a sense, this has been recognised by those who constructively oppose 'globalisation', pointing to and posing alternatives to what are taken to be its deleterious manifestations. Such views remain limited to the extent that capitalism is *merely understood as globalisation*, from which all its evil consequences can be easily read off and, in principle, corrected. However, globalisation, in whatever aspect and however understood, should be seen as the *effect* of capitalism's international reproduction and, consequently, *the form taken by the laws of political economy in the current period*. In short, whatever meaning is to be attached to globalisation in its application across economic, political and ideological aspects, its fundamental attachment to the production and appropriation of surplus value needs to be sustained analytically.

Capital's Environment

Consider now the problem of environmental degradation. Here Marxism has been accused of privileging the social at the expense of the natural, underestimating the potential for reform, and even of precluding consideration of the natural because of excessive preoccupation with the economic. Whilst Marx had much to say about what we would now term the 'environment', he only rarely addressed it directly. But his theories of commodity fetishism and of the labour process offer excellent insights into his simultaneous emphasis upon both social *and* material factors, as value and use value production. This offers an appropriate approach to the environment. It should be understood first and foremost in terms of environmental *relations* (and corresponding structures and conflicts) characteristic of *capitalism*. This contrasts with the idea of a trans-historical conflict between ecological and social systems, or between the environment and the economy. However, these environmental relations are driven by capitalist relations of production. Thus, as is readily recognised, the drive for profitability leads, through the rising organic composition of capital, to the working up of ever more raw materials into commodities and the corresponding extraction and use of energy and minerals, without immediate regard to their environmental impact.

Yet, capitalism is also capable, not least through the development of new materials and through state regulation, of tempering or even reversing at least partly such environmental degradation. In this respect, it is important to recognise the multi-dimensional nature of the environment and the diverse range of issues and outcomes involved, from pollution through bio-technology to drugs, vaccines and artificial body parts. Again, the lessons to be drawn from commodity fetishism are significant. Marx argues that commodity relations appear primarily as what they really are, social relations expressed as relations between things, and as monetary magnitudes. What is not apparent are the underlying class relations of exploitation, the dynamics to which they give rise, and the reasons for these. By the same token, how commodities have been created as use values, with their corresponding attachment to the environment, is no more revealed to us than the geographical origins of the commodity or its dependence (or not) on sweated or child labour, unless these be overtly deployed, legitimately or not, as a selling point.

Not surprisingly, these 'hidden' aspects of the commodity, and its systems of production, distribution and exchange, are inevitably brought to our attention, inducing reactions against them. Struggles against child labour, to reveal its incidence and to campaign against it at the point of production through to point of sale, are after all directed at the *nature* of humanity and its reproduction in material and cultural respects. By the same token, the reproduction of environmental relations, optimistically dubbed 'sustainability', is inevitably a shifting confrontation with a range of aspects of capitalist commodity relations. As long as these relations persist, so will the system of production to which they are attached, with the corresponding tendencies to appropriate and transform the environment, however much this may be tempered by regulation that tends to be obstructed or evaded by competitive pressures.

Socialism

What is socialism and does it offer better prospects in social, environmental and other respects? Socialist experiments in the twentieth century closely associated themselves with Marx(ism), and have been seen as Marxist in popular understanding. However, long before the collapse of the Eastern European bloc, controversy had long raged among Marxists over the nature of the Soviet Union, with stances ranging from uncritical support to condemnation as (state) capitalism.

In the event, the Soviet Union, over what is in relative terms a brief historical period, has gone through a remarkable transformation, well captured in Marx's notion of primitive accumulation. For what was primarily a semi-feudal society, with a large proportion of its workforce in agriculture, has succeeded in creating at breakneck speed a wage labour market and (at least until recently) a relatively advanced and well-integrated industrial base. The last decade has witnessed the completion of this transition through the re-emergence of private property in major means of production and a class of capitalists. Some have argued that such an end result was inevitable, given the low initial productive base and relentless international hostility faced by the Soviet Union throughout its history. Even so, the pace, direction and consequences of such a transition to capitalism are far from predetermined, as is evidenced by the (as yet) less cataclysmic, if equally dramatic, adoption of 'market forces' in China.

Thus, whilst Marx is well known for his criticisms of capitalism as an exploitative system, he is probably more thought of as having inspired failed and possibly failing twentieth-century attempts at constructing socialism. Even though there is little work by Marx dealing directly and exclusively with the economics of socialism, contrary to much opinion, Marx does have much to say on the topic, not least in the *Critique of the Gotha Programme*. Generally, he is less interested in designing utopian blueprints than drawing upon, and extrapolating from, developments within capitalism itself, proceeding in two separate but closely related ways.

First, he sees capitalism as increasingly socialising life – through the organisation of production, the economy more generally, and through state power – but in ways that are fundamentally constrained by the private nature of the market, private property and the imperative of profitability. Competition tends to socialise capitalist production through the increasingly intricate division of labour on the shopfloor, and in society as a whole. In addition to this, the increasing role of the state in welfare provision, redistribution and production itself through planning or nationalised industries for example, all anticipate some of the economic and social forms of a future socialism. The same applies to the formation of worker co-operatives and so on, with or without state support. Yet these embryonic forms are inevitably constrained in content, form and even survival by their confinement within capitalist society, the direct or indirect imperatives of profitability, and the economic and social system that depends upon it. Some forms of socialisation – the planning of production within large-scale firms to the exclusion of the market, or the broader and deeper role of money through the financial system – have a very different affinity to socialism than the provision of health, education and welfare through the state. In this respect, the popular slogan 'People before Profit' expresses socialist values within an acceptance of capitalism since profit is allowed as long as it is not privileged. Here there is a neat correspondence with Marx's critique of Proudhon's notion that 'Property Is Theft', for it both condemns and accepts property (without which there cannot be theft).

Second, then, Marx's anticipation of socialism derives from the contradictions within capitalism, irrespective of whether these have evolved into embryonic socialist forms. Most notable is the revolutionary role to be played by the working class – with capitalism creating, expanding, strengthening and organising labour for the purposes of production, but necessarily exploiting the working majority and failing to meet its broader economic and social aspirations. In the telling phrase of the *Communist Manifesto*, 'what the bourgeoisie ... produces, above all, is its own grave-diggers. Its fall and the victory of the proletariat are equally inevitable.'

Such is the means for socialist revolution. Motivation arises out of the various aspects of exploitation, alienation and human debasement characteristic of capitalism and how they may be superseded. Under capitalism, the working class is deprived of control of the production process, of its results in products themselves, and of comprehensive knowledge of, and influence upon, the workings of society and its development. The workers are also subjected to severe limitations in their prospects and potential achievements, and continuous upheaval in their living conditions, whose fortunes shift with the ebb and flow of the profit imperative and fortunes of the economy. This is highly wasteful both in economic and, more importantly, in human terms. This has led to workplace resistance and political confrontation and, historically, this has provided a powerful stimulus for social reforms and anti-capitalist rebellion.

For Marx, the abolition of capitalism marks the end of the prehistory of human society. However, the transition to communism is neither inexorable nor unavoidable. The social relations at the core of capitalism will change only if overwhelming pressure is applied by the majority. Failing that, capitalism may persist indefinitely, in spite of its rising human and environmental costs. Nonetheless, the passage to socialism can only be achieved in stages rather than being magically completed on demand, with its first phase being marked by the continuing influence of the heavy historical baggage of capitalism. Marx argues that, at a later stage, when the division of labour and the opposition between mental and manual labour have been overcome, and the development of the productive forces has reached a level that is sufficiently high to permit the all-round development of the individuals, the advanced phase of socialism (communism) can be reached. As he put it in the *Critique of the Gotha Programme*, 'from each according to his ability, to each according to his needs!'

Such prognoses stand shoulder to shoulder with the slogan that marks Marx's epitaph, the eleventh thesis on Feuerbach: 'The philosophers have only *interpreted* the world, in various ways; the point is to *change* it.' As with much of Marx's writings, this call to nineteenth-century socialists should be interpreted both as a means of gaining understanding as well as an imperative to act. It remains fully valid into the twenty-first century.

Issues and Further Reading

Outstanding Marxian studies of class include Geoffrey de Ste. Croix (1984) and Ellen Wood (1998); for a recent collection of essays, see *Socialist Register* (2001). Marxian theories of the state are reviewed by Ben Fine and Laurence Harris (1979, chs 6, 9); see also Suzanne de Brunhoff (1978), Paul Cammack (1989), Simon Clarke (1991), Bob Jessop (1982) and Ellen Wood (1981, 1991, 2003).

Capitalist 'globalisation' is discussed in a vast literature. This section draws on Ben Fine (2002, ch. 2) and Alfredo Saad-Filho (2003a); see also Hugo Radice (1999, 2000) and John Weeks (2001). Another set of Marxian studies refers specifically to imperialism; see, for example, Anthony Brewer (1989), Norman Etherington (1984), Eric Hobsbawm (1987) and recent issues of the *Monthly Review*.

There is a growing Marxian literature on the environment and environmental crisis. See, for example, Ted Benton (1996), Finn Bowring (2003), Paul Burkett (1999, 2003), John Bellamy Foster (1999, 2000, 2002) and Les Levidow (2003). The journal *Capitalism, Nature, Socialism* includes a wealth of material, but see also the special issue of *Capital & Class* (72, 2000).

Marx's comments on socialism and communism can be found mainly in Karl Marx (1974) and Karl Marx and Friedrich Engels (1998); see also Friedrich Engels (1998, part 3). This chapter draws upon Ben Fine (1983b). Current debates about socialism are reviewed by Paresh Chattopadhyay (2003), Duncan Foley (1986, ch. 10), Michael Lebowitz (2003b) and Dimitris Milonakis (2003), but see also Michael Perelman (2000) and the special issues of *Science & Society* (66: 1, 2002) and *Socialist Register* (2000). The Soviet experience is critically discussed, from different viewpoints, by Chris Arthur (2002, ch. 10), Paresh Chattopadhyay (1994) and Simon Clarke (2003). The journal *Critique* has published extensively on this issue.

References

Many of Karl Marx's works are freely available on the internet. See, for example, the Marxists Internet Archive <http://www.marxists.org/>, the MarX-Files <http://www.prestat.appstate.edu/~stanovskydj/marxfiles.html> and the Akamac home page <http://www.cpm.ll.ehime-u.ac.jp/AkamacHomePage/Akamac_E-text_Links/Akamac_E-text_Links.html>.

Arthur, C. (2001) 'Value, Labour and Negativity', *Capital and Class* 73, pp. 15–39.

Arthur, C. (2002) *The New Dialectic and Marx's 'Capital'*. Leiden: Brill Academic Publishers.

Arthur, C. and Reuten, G. (eds) (1998) *The Circulation of Capital: Essays on Volume Two of 'Capital'*. London: Macmillan.

Ashton, T.H. and Philpin, C.H.E. (eds) (1985) *The Brenner Debate: Agrarian Class Structure and Economic Development in Pre-Industrial Europe*. Cambridge: Cambridge University Press.

Benton, T. (ed.) (1996) *The Greening of Marxism*. London: The Guilford Press.

Bina, C. (1989) 'Some Controversies in the Development of Rent Theory: The Nature of Oil Rent', *Capital and Class* 39, pp. 82–112.

Bleaney, M. (1976) *Underconsumption Theories: A History and Critical Analysis*. London: Lawrence & Wishart.

Bottomore, T. (ed.) (1991) *A Dictionary of Marxist Thought*. Oxford: Basil Blackwell.

Bowring, F. (2003) 'Manufacturing Scarcity: Food Biotechnology and the Life-Sciences Industry', *Capital and Class* 79, pp. 107–44.

Brenner, R. (1986) 'The Social Basis of Economic Development', in J. Roemer (ed.) *Analytical Marxism*. Cambridge: Cambridge University Press.

Brenner, R. (1998) 'The Economics of Global Turbulence', *New Left Review* 229, pp. 1–265.
Brenner, R. (2002) *The Boom and the Bubble: The U.S. in the World Economy*. London: Verso.
Brewer, A. (1989) *Marxist Theories of Imperialism: A Critical Survey*. London: Routledge.
Brighton Labour Process Group (1977) 'The Capitalist Labour Process', *Capital and Class* 1, pp. 3–26.
Brunhoff, S. de (1976) *Marx on Money*. New York: Urizen Books.
Brunhoff, S. de (1978) *The State, Capital and Economic Policy*. London: Pluto Press.
Brunhoff, S. de (2003) 'Financial and Industrial Capital: A New Class Coalition', in A. Saad-Filho (ed.) *Anti-Capitalism: A Marxist Introduction*. London: Pluto Press.
Burkett, P. (1999) *Marx and Nature: A Red and Green Perspective*. New York: St Martin's Press.
Burkett, P. (2003) 'Capitalism, Nature and the Class Struggle', in A. Saad-Filho (ed.) *Anti-Capitalism: A Marxist Introduction*. London: Pluto Press.
Byres, T. (1996) *Capitalism from Above and Capitalism from Below*. London: Macmillan.
Cammack, P. (1989) 'Bringing the State Back In?' *British Journal of Political Science* 19 (2), pp. 261–90.
Chattopadhyay, P. (1994) *The Marxian Concept of Capital and the Soviet Experience: Essay in the Critique of Political Economy*. Westport, Conn.: Praeger.
Chattopadhyay, P. (2003) 'Towards a Society of Free and Associated Individuals: Communism', in A. Saad-Filho (ed.) *Anti-Capitalism: A Marxist Introduction*. London: Pluto Press.
Clarke, S. (ed.) (1991) *The State Debate*. London: CSE/Macmillan.
Clarke, S. (1994) *Marx's Theory of Crisis*. London: Macmillan.
Clarke, S. (2003) 'Globalisation and the Subsumption of the Soviet Mode of Production under Capital', in A. Saad-Filho (ed.) *Anti-Capitalism: A Marxist Introduction*. London: Pluto Press.
Duménil, G. (1980) *De la Valeur aux Prix de Production*. Paris: Economica.
Elson, D. (1979) 'The Value Theory of Labour', in *Value, The Representation of Labour in Capitalism*. London: CSE Books.

Engels, F. (1998) *Anti-Dühring*, in K. Marx and F. Engels, *Classics in Politics* (CD-Rom). London: The Electric Book Company.
Etherington, N. (1984) *Theories of Imperialism: War, Conquest and Capital*. London: Croom Helm.
Fine, B. (1980) *Economic Theory and Ideology*. London: Edward Arnold.
Fine, B. (1982) *Theories of the Capitalist Economy*. London: Edward Arnold.
Fine, B. (1983a) 'A Dissenting Note on the Transformation Problem', *Economy and Society* 12 (4), pp. 520–25.
Fine, B. (1983b) 'Marx on Economic Relations under Socialism', in B. Matthews (ed.) *Marx: A Hundred Years On*. London: Lawrence & Wishart.
Fine, B. (1985–86) 'Banking Capital and the Theory of Interest', *Science and Society*, 49 (4), pp. 387–413.
Fine, B. (ed.) (1986) *The Value Dimension, Marx versus Ricardo and Sraffa*. London: Routledge and Kegan Paul.
Fine, B. (1988) 'From Capital in Production to Capital in Exchange', *Science and Society* 52 (3), pp. 326–37.
Fine, B. (1990a) 'On the Composition of Capital, A Comment on Groll and Orzech', *History of Political Economy* 22 (1), pp. 149–55.
Fine, B. (1990b) *The Coal Question: Political Economy and Industrial Change from the Nineteenth Century to the Present Day*. London: Routledge.
Fine, B. (1992a) 'On the Falling Rate of Profit', in G.A. Caravale (ed.) *Marx and Modern Economic Analysis*. Aldershot: Edward Elgar.
Fine, B. (1992b) *Women's Employment and the Capitalist Family*. London: Routledge.
Fine, B. (1998) *Labour Market Theory: A Constructive Reassessment*. London: Routledge.
Fine, B. (2001a) 'The Continuing Imperative of Value Theory', *Capital and Class* 75, pp. 41–52.
Fine, B. (2001b) *Social Capital versus Social Theory*. London: Routledge.
Fine, B. (2002) *The World of Consumption: The Material and Cultural Revisited* (2nd edn). London: Routledge.
Fine, B. (2003) 'Contesting Labour Markets', in A. Saad-Filho (ed.) *Anti-Capitalism: A Marxist Introduction*. London: Pluto Press.

Fine, B. and Harris, L. (1979) *Rereading Capital*. London: Macmillan.
Fine, B., Heasman, M. and Wright, J. (1996) *Consumption in the Age of Affluence*. London: Routledge.
Fine, B. and Leopold, E. (1993) *The World of Consumption*. London: Routledge.
Fine, B., Lapavitsas, C. and Milonakis, D. (1999) 'Addressing the World Economy: Two Steps Back', *Capital and Class* 67, pp. 47–90.
Fine, B., Lapavitsas, C. and Saad-Filho, A. (2004) 'Transforming the Transformation Problem: Why the "New Interpretation" is a Wrong Turning', *Review of Radical Political Economics*, forthcoming.
Foley, D. (1982) 'The Value of Money, the Value of Labour Power and the Marxian Transformation Problem', *Review of Radical Political Economics* 14 (2), pp. 37–47.
Foley, D. (1986) *Understanding Capital, Marx's Economic Theory*. Cambridge, Mass.: Harvard University Press.
Foley, D. (2000) 'Recent Developments in the Labor Theory of Value', *Review of Radical Political Economics* 32 (1), pp. 1–39.
Foster, J.B. (1999) *The Vulnerable Planet*. New York: Monthly Review Press.
Foster, J.B. (2000) *Marx's Ecology*. New York: Monthly Review Press.
Foster, J.B. (2002) *Ecology Against Capitalism*. New York: Monthly Review Press.
Guerrero, D. (2003) 'Capitalist Competition and the Distribution of Profits', in A. Saad-Filho (ed.) *Anti-Capitalism: A Marxist Introduction*. London: Pluto Press.
Harvey, D. (1999) *The Limits to Capital*. London: Verso.
Hilferding, R. (1981) *Finance Capital*. London: Routledge and Kegan Paul.
Hilton, R. (1976) *The Transition from Feudalism to Capitalism*. London: New Left Books.
Hobsbawm, E. (1987) *Age of Empire*. London: Weidenfeld and Nicolson.
Howard, M.C. and King, J.E. (1989, 1991) *A History of Marxian Economics*, 2 Vols. London: Macmillan.
Howard, M.C. and King, J.E. (1990) 'The "Second Slump": Marxian Theories of Crisis after 1973', *Review of Political Economy* 2 (3), pp. 267–91.

Itoh, M. and Lapavitsas, C. (1999) *Political Economy of Money and Finance*. London: Macmillan.

Jessop, B. (1982) *The Capitalist State: Marxist Theories and Methods*. Oxford: Robertson.

Lapavitsas, C. (2000a) 'Money and the Analysis of Capitalism: The Significance of Commodity Money', *Review of Radical Political Economics* 32 (4), pp. 631–56.

Lapavitsas, C. (2000b) 'On Marx's Analysis of Money Hoarding in the Turnover of Capital', *Review of Political Economy* 12 (2), pp. 219–35.

Lapavitsas, C. (2003a) 'Money as Money and Money as Capital in a Capitalist Economy', in A. Saad-Filho (ed.) *Anti-Capitalism: A Marxist Introduction*. London: Pluto Press.

Lapavitsas, C. (2003b) *Social Foundations of Markets, Money and Credit*. London: Routledge.

Lapavitsas, C. and Saad-Filho, A. (2000) 'The Supply of Credit Money and Capital Accumulation: A Critical View of Post-Keynesian Analysis', *Research in Political Economy* 18, pp. 309–34.

Lapides, K. (1998) *Marx's Wage Theory in Historical Perspective*. Westport, Conn.: Praeger.

Lebowitz, M. (2003a) *Beyond 'Capital': Marx's Political Economy of the Working Class* (2nd edn). London: Palgrave.

Lebowitz, M. (2003b) 'Transcending Capitalism: The Adequacy of Marx's Recipe', in A. Saad-Filho (ed.) *Anti-Capitalism: A Marxist Introduction*. London: Pluto Press.

Lenin, V.I. (1972) *The Development of Capitalism in Russia*, Collected Works, Vol. 3. London: Lawrence & Wishart.

Levidow, L. (2003), 'Technological Change as Class Struggle', in A. Saad-Filho (ed.) *Anti-Capitalism: A Marxist Introduction*. London: Pluto Press.

Levidow, L. and Young, B. (1981, 1985) *Science, Technology and the Labour Process, Marxist Studies*, 2 Vols. London: Free Association Books.

Marglin, S. (1974) 'What Do Bosses Do?', *Review of Radical Political Economics* 6 (2), pp. 60–112.

Marx, K. (1969, 1972, 1978a) *Theories of Surplus Value*, 3 Vols. London: Lawrence & Wishart.

Marx, K. (1974) 'Critique of the Gotha Programme', in *The First International and After*. Harmondsworth: Penguin.

Marx, K. (1976, 1978b, 1981a) *Capital*, 3 Vols. Harmondsworth: Penguin.

Marx, K. (1981b) *Grundrisse*. Harmondsworth: Penguin.

Marx, K. (1987) *A Contribution to the Critique of Political Economy*, Collected Works, Vol. 29. London: Lawrence & Wishart.

Marx, K. (1998) *Value, Price and Profit*, in K. Marx and F. Engels, *Classics in Politics* (CD-Rom). London: The Electric Book Company.

Marx, K. and Engels, F. (1998) *The Communist Manifesto*, in K. Marx and F. Engels, *Classics in Politics* (CD-Rom). London: The Electric Book Company.

McLellan, D. (1974) *Karl Marx: His Life and Thought*. London: Macmillan.

Medio, A. (1977) 'Neoclassicals, Neo-Ricardians, and Marx', in J. Schwartz (ed.) *The Subtle Anatomy of Capitalism*. Santa Monica: Goodyear.

Milonakis, D. (2003) 'New Market Socialism: A Case for Rejuvenation or Inspired Alchemy?', *Cambridge Journal of Economics* 27, pp. 97–121.

Mohun, S. (ed.) (1995) *Debates in Value Theory*. London: Macmillan.

Mohun, S. (2003) 'Does All Labour Create Value?', in A. Saad-Filho (ed.) *Anti-Capitalism: A Marxist Introduction*. London: Pluto Press.

Moseley, F. (ed.) (1993) *Marx's Method in 'Capital', A Reexamination*. Atlantic Highlands, N.J.: Humanities Press.

Oakley, A. (1983) *The Making of Marx's Critical Theory*. London: Routledge and Kegan Paul.

Oakley, A. (1984, 1985) *Marx's Critique of Political Economy, Intellectual Sources and Evolution*, 2 Vols. London: Routledge and Kegan Paul.

Okishio, N. (1961) 'Technical Change and the Rate of Profit', *Kobe University Economic Review* 7, pp. 85–99.

Okishio, N. (2000) 'Competition and Production Prices', *Cambridge Journal of Economics* 25, pp. 493–501.

Perelman, M. (1987) *Marx's Crises Theory: Scarcity, Labor, and Finance*. Westport, Conn.: Praeger.

Perelman, M. (2000) *Transcending the Economy: On the Potential of Passionate Labour and the Wastes of the Market.* New York: St Martin's Press.

Perelman, M. (2003) 'The History of Capitalism', in A. Saad-Filho (ed.) *Anti-Capitalism: A Marxist Introduction.* London: Pluto Press.

Pilling, G. (1980) *Marx's* Capital: *Philosophy and Political Economy.* London: Routledge and Kegan Paul.

Postone, M. (1993) *Time, Labour and Social Domination, A Re-examination of Marx's Critical Theory.* Cambridge: Cambridge University Press.

Radice, H. (1999) 'Taking Globalisation Seriously', *Socialist Register,* pp. 1–28.

Radice, H. (2000) 'Globalization and National Capitalism: Theorizing Convergence and Differentiation', *Review of International Political Economy* 7 (4), pp. 719–42.

Reuten, G. (1997) 'The Notion of Tendency in Marx's 1894 Law of Profit', in F. Moseley and M. Campbell (eds) *New Investigations of Marx's Method.* Atlantic Highlands, N.J.: Humanities Press.

Rosdolsky, R. (1977) *The Making of Marx's 'Capital'.* London: Pluto Press.

Rosenthal, J. (1997) *The Myth of Dialectics: Reinterpreting the Marx–Hegel Relation.* London: Macmillan.

Rowthorn, B. (1980) *Capitalism, Conflict and Inflation.* London: Lawrence & Wishart.

Rubin, I.I. (1975) *Essays on Marx's Theory of Value.* Montréal: Black Rose Books.

Rubin, I.I. (1979) *A History of Economic Thought.* London: Pluto Press.

Saad-Filho, A. (1993) 'A Note on Marx's Analysis of the Composition of Capital', *Capital and Class* 50, pp. 127–46.

Saad-Filho, A. (1996) 'The Value of Money, the Value of Labour Power and the Net Product: An Appraisal of the "New Solution" to the Transformation Problem', in A. Freeman and G. Carchedi (eds) *Marx and Non-Equilibrium Economics.* Aldershot: Edward Elgar.

Saad-Filho, A. (1997a) 'Concrete and Abstract Labour in Marx's Theory of Value', *Review of Political Economy* 9 (4), pp. 457–77.

Saad-Filho, A. (1997b) 'An Alternative Reading of the Transformation of Values into Prices of Production', *Capital and Class* 63, pp. 115–36.

Saad-Filho, A. (2001) 'Capital Accumulation and the Composition of Capital', *Research in Political Economy* 19, pp. 69–85.

Saad-Filho, A. (2002) *The Value of Marx: Political Economy for Contemporary Capitalism*. London: Routledge.

Saad-Filho, A. (2003a) 'Introduction', in A. Saad-Filho (ed.) *Anti-Capitalism: A Marxist Introduction*. London: Pluto Press.

Saad-Filho, A. (2003b) 'Value, Capital and Exploitation', in A. Saad-Filho (ed.) *Anti-Capitalism: A Marxist Introduction*. London: Pluto Press.

Savran, S. and Tonak, A. (1999) 'Productive and Unproductive Labour: an Attempt at Clarification and Classification', *Capital and Class*, 68, pp. 113–52.

Schwartz, J. (ed.) (1977) *The Subtle Anatomy of Capitalism*. Santa Monica: Goodyear.

Scott, S. (1999) 'Thought and Social Struggle: A History of Dialectics'. PhD Thesis, University of Bradford.

Shaikh, A. (1978) 'A History of Crisis Theories', in URPE (ed.) *US Capitalism in Crisis*. New York: URPE.

Shaikh, A. (1981) 'The Poverty of Algebra', in I. Steedman (ed.) *The Value Controversy*. London: Verso.

Shaikh, A. (1982) 'Neo-Ricardian Economics, a Wealth of Algebra, a Poverty of Theory', *Review of Radical Political Economics* 14 (2), pp. 67–83.

Slater, P. (ed.) (1980) *Outlines of a Critique of Technology*. Atlantic Highlands, N.J.: Humanities Press.

Smith, T. (1990) *The Logic of Marx's 'Capital', Reply to Hegelian Criticisms*. Albany: State of New York Press.

Ste. Croix, G. de (1984) 'Class in Marx's Conception of History, Ancient and Modern', *New Left Review* 146, pp. 94–111.

Steedman, I. (1977) *Marx after Sraffa*. London: New Left Books.

Wajcman, J. (2002) 'Addressing Technological Change: The Challenge to Social Theory', *Current Sociology* 50 (3), pp. 347–64.

Weeks, J. (1981) *Capital and Exploitation*. Princeton: Princeton University Press.

Weeks, J. (1982a) 'Equilibrium, Uneven Development and the Tendency of the Rate of Profit to Fall', *Capital and Class* 16, pp. 62–77.

Weeks, J. (1982b) 'A Note on Underconsumptionist Theory and the Labor Theory of Value', *Science and Society* 46 (1), pp. 60–76.

Weeks, J. (1983) 'On the Issue of Capitalist Circulation and the Concepts Appropriate to Its Analysis', *Science and Society* 48 (2), pp. 214–25.

Weeks, J. (1985–86) 'Epochs of Capitalism and the Progressiveness of Capital's Expansion', *Science and Society* 49 (4), pp. 414–35.

Weeks, J. (1990) 'Abstract Labor and Commodity Production', *Research in Political Economy* 12, pp. 3–19.

Weeks, J. (2001) 'The Expansion of Capital and Uneven Development on a World Scale', *Capital and Class* 74, pp. 9–30.

Wheen, F. (2000) *Karl Marx*. London: Fourth Estate.

Wood, E.M. (1981) 'The Separation of the Economic and the Political in Capitalism, *New Left Review* 127, May–June, pp. 66–95.

Wood, E.M. (1984) 'Marxism and the Course of History', *New Left Review* 147, pp. 95–107.

Wood, E.M. (1991) *The Pristine Culture of Capitalism*. London: Verso.

Wood, E.M. (1998) *The Retreat from Class: A New 'True' Socialism*. London: Verso.

Wood, E.M. (2002) *The Origin of Capitalism: A Longer View*. London: Verso.

Wood, E.M. (2003) 'Globalisation and the State: Where Is the Power of Capital?', in A. Saad-Filho (ed.) *Anti-Capitalism: A Marxist Introduction*. London: Pluto Press.

Index

Abstinence 29, 38
Accumulation of capital 41, 44, 54, 57–8, 61, 63–5, 68–9, 72, 74–88, 89–91, 95–100, 104, 106–7, 110–13, 115–21, 124–5, 133, 143–4, 147–9, 151, 153–4, 158, 160, 163–5, 168, 172
  primitive 74–9, 87, 176
  see also capital
Advertising 26
Agent, economic 82, 85, 100, 135–6
Alienation 26, 28–9, 178
Analysis, levels 7, 9, 159
Anti-capitalism 179
Arthur, C. 12–13, 48, 60, 180
Ashton, T.H. 87

Balance of payments 150
Banking capital *see* interest-bearing capital
Banking system 67,145–6, 151, *see also* credit, finance
Bankruptcy 27, 83, 94, 99, 118–19
Barter 31
Benton, T. 180
Bina, C. 165
Bleaney, M. 101
Bottomore, T. 12
Bowring, F. 180
Brenner, R. 87, 101
Brewer, A. 180
Brighton Labour Process Group 49
Brunhoff, S. de 152, 180
Bubbles *see* speculation
Burkett, P. 180
Business cycle 96
Byres, T. 87

Cammack, P. 180
Capital
  advanced 52–3, 75, 80, 96, 127, 129, 132–3, 137–8, 142
  aim to produce social use value 20–1
  centralisation 86–7, 99, 117, 144
  commercial 8, 47–8, 51, 56, 126–7, 136–8, 143, 145
  commodity capital 54–5, 57–8, 92, 143
  commodity circuit of 57, 59
  concentration 85–7, 117
  constant 40–1, 61, 96, 104–6, 115, 124, 127, 163
  devaluation 117
  fixed 40, 46, 51, 82, 94, 96, 99, 118, 121, 127
  in general 83
  industrial circuit of 52–4, 139, 142–4

Capital *continued*
migration 85, 129–30, 149
money circuit of 51–3, 56–7, 59
productive circuit of 53, 57, 59
self-expanding value 35–6, 52–4, 87, 142
social xiv
turnover 51
variable 40, 61, 96, 104, 106, 115, 124, 127, 129, 132, 137–8, 154
as a whole 52–60, 61, 65–6, 70, 72, 89–94, 117, 136, 147
see also accumulation of capital, capitalism, exchange, means of production, production, surplus value, value of labour power, wage
Capitalism
abolition v, 179
contemporary xiii–xv, 9, 25, 27, 145, 152
division of labour 137, 177
main features 4–11, 15–29, 31, 33–4, 36–40, 42–6, 51–4, 56–9, 61–4, 68–71, 74–7, 81–2, 86–96, 97–100, 102–3, 106–7, 110, 119, 126–7, 169
mass production 87
see also capital, competition, exploitation, manufacture, mechanisation, production, relations of production, reproduction
Capital–labour ratio 21
Central bank 67
Chattopadhyay, P. 88, 181
Circulation period *see* capital, turnover
Circulation *see* exchange
Clarke, S. 101, 180–1
Class
analysis v, 6, 10, 13, 16, 24, 26, 29, 52, 58, 67, 69, 87, 99, 107, 164, 167–72, 175, 180
capitalist 6, 10, 23–4, 26, 39, 43, 76, 78, 99–101, 143, 148, 151, 170–1, 176
conflict or struggle v, 89, 107, 167
landowning 126
middle 169
ruling 171
working 1, 23–4, 37, 42–5, 72–3, 76–81, 100, 167, 170–1, 178, 180
see also exploitation
Classical political economy 11, 96–7, 150
Commodity
agricultural 161–2
circulation, equivalence or exchange 17–18, 22, 32–4, 52, 62, 65, 119, 135
concept 16–19, 23, 175
economy or society 16, 19, 21, 31, 46, 62, 65, 137, 175
fetishism 4, 25–9, 174–5
form 9, 18–20, 29, 31
form of non-products of labour 19
simple production 22, 31, 34, 136
value and price 9, 20–2, 32, 40–1, 64, 84–5, 95, 97, 103–4, 106–7, 113, 120–2, 130–3, 138, 155
see also capital, exchange, price, value

Communism xv, 8–9, 28, 99–100, 166, 176–81
Communist Manifesto, The 8, 178
Competition
and accumulation 20, 26, 44, 69, 76, 80, 82–3, 86–8, 89, 91, 95, 98–9, 107, 112, 120, 125–6, 144, 171, 177
in agriculture 151, 157, 161, 163–4
between industrial and interest-bearing capital 144, 149, 151
international 27
inter-sectoral 83–6, 112, 119, 132, 149, 161
intra-sectoral 83–4, 86, 95, 99, 110, 112, 119
see also technical change
Composition of capital, organic (OCC) 104–8, 110–14, 118, 120, 123–4, 129–30, 132–4, 155, 161–5, 174
technical (TCC) 46, 97, 102–8
value (VCC) 104–8, 110, 113–14, 118, 120, 123–4, 129–30, 132–4
Concepts 28, 39, 109
derivation and introduction 1–4, 6–8, 12, 15, 64
see also analysis
Consumption 10, 16–7, 27, 32–4, 38, 49, 53, 57–9, 61–3, 65–6, 72, 84, 90, 93, 95, 100, 125, 135, 150–1, 153
productive 40, 120
Contingency 7, 21, 46–7, 121, 160, 164, 168–9
Contradiction 2, 4–5, 7, 45, 85, 89–91, 95, 107, 111, 114–15, 117, 119, 121, 155, 178
Co-operation 43, 82, 177
Counter-tendency 7, 84, *see also* contingency, law, tendency, trend
Craft work 45, 82
Credit 69, 79, 86–7, 93, 119, 136, 143–5, 151–2
commercial or trade 96, 169
system 20, 47–8, 69, 72, 83, 86, 90, 94, 143–9, 151, 169, 178
see also banking system, finance, financial assets, financial capital, interest-bearing capital, money
Crisis 27–8, 69–70, 89–91, 94–5, 99–101, 117–19, 122, 124–5
environmental 180
financial xiv, 69
see also disproportionality, overproduction, underconsumption

Demand and supply 21, 59, 66, 85, 90, 92–3, 96, 116
land 153
loanable money capital 150
interest-bearing capital 143
money 147–8, 150
Departments 1 and 2 61–3, 65
Depreciation 118, 127
Deskilling 45, 99, *see also* labour
Dialectics 2–5, 7, 12, 111, 123
Disequilibrium 124, 151
Disproportionality 66, 83, 92–3, 95–6, 117, *see also* crisis
Distribution, capital 54, 85, 126, 159
income 51
labour 85, 126
products 11, 18, 20, 51

Distribution, capital *continued*
relations 10, 16, 22, 24, 56, 58, 67–9, 76, 101, 126, 173, 175, 177
net product or value added 56, 68
surplus value or profit 54, 85, 126–7, 129, 133, 137, 139, 158, 162
theory 56
see also exploitation
Dividends 57, 127
Division of labour 15, 19, 43, 137, 177, 179, *see also* capitalism, labour, production
Duménil, G. 134

Economic growth 28, 78, 97, 119, *see also* growth theory, productivity
Economic reproduction
expanded 54, 59, 61, 63–70, 86, 90–1, 93, 146
individual 10
simple 61–3, 91
social 10, 15, 17, 19, 22, 39, 49, 58, 61, 70–3, 81, 88, 169, 172, 175
workers 42, 44, 58, 73, 98, 116, 170, 172
Efficiency 16, 42, 76, 80, 82–4, 99, 136, 153, 168, *see also* productivity
Elson, D. 30
Employment 11, 27, 42, 47, 65–6, 76, 81, 92, 96–8, 151, 172, *see also* labour, reserve army, unemployment
Enclosure movement 76, 78
Engels, F. v, 9, 30, 181
Environment xiv, 26–7, 167, 174–6, 179–80, *see also* nature
Equilibrium 59, 64–6, 85, 111–12, 122–4, 133, 148, 151, *see also* reproduction
Essence 4, 7, 16, 19–20, 28, 74, 79, *see also* dialectics
Etherington, N. 180
Exchange rate 145, 172
Exchange value, *see* value
Exchange
commodity 32, 34, 55–7, 92, 111, 113, 115, 117, 126, 135, 136, 138, 146, 169, 172
equal 37
unequal 32, 37, 133
see also commodity
Exploitation
capitalist 4, 6, 25–7, 36–40, 47–9, 81, 91–2, 113, 116, 140, 175, 177–8
class 26, 175
distribution, feudal 25
international 78
modes 6
rate 39–41
unproductive workers 47
see also capitalism, distribution, feudalism, slavery, surplus value, wage

Factory system 21, 40, 45–6, 48, 81–2, 97, 102
Feudalism 5–6, 8, 10, 18, 25, 39, 75–6, 80, 87, *see also* exploitation
Finance xiv, 91, 101, 121, 123, 139, 144, 147, 149–50, 152, 154, 173, *see also* banking system, credit, crisis,

financial assets, financial capital
Financial assets, instruments or investment 36, 57, 144, *see also* finance, financial capital, stock market
Financial capital 69, 126 *see also* finance, financial assets
Financial institutions, sector or system *see* credit system
Fine, B. xvi, 12, 29–30, 48–50, 60, 73, 88, 101, 108, 125, 134, 141, 152, 165, 180–1
Fiscal deficits 118
Foley, D. 13, 30, 48, 101, 125, 134, 141, 152, 181
Forces of production 86, *see also* mode of production, production
Foster, J.B. 180

Globalisation xiv, 27, 101, 166, 171–4, 180
Growth theory 59, 64, *see also* economic growth
Guerrero, D. 88

Harris, L. 50, 101, 108, 125, 180
Harvey, D. 30, 48, 60, 88, 101, 152, 165
Heasman, M. 73
Hegel, G.W.F. 1–2, 4
  Hegel's method 2, 4, 6–7, 13, 28
  see also dialectics, Idea
Hilferding, R. 152
Hilton, R. 87
Hobsbawm, E. 180
Household production 16, 71, 80
Howard, M.C. 12, 101

Idea 2, *see also* Hegel's method
Idealism 1, 6, 28
Ideology xv, 3, 15, 27, 29, 58 66–7, 98, 100, 167, 170, 172, 174
Imperialism 180
Industrial reserve army *see* reserve army
Inflation 76
Interest v, 27, 48, 57, 127, 133, 135, 142–3, 145, 148–52
  rate 59, 67, 142, 148–51
Interest-bearing capital (IBC) 48, 51, 56, 135, 140, 142–52, *see also* credit, finance
Investment 53, 61, 66, 84, 86, 92–3, 95, 99, 117–18, 126, 154, 156, 158–9, 161 163, 168
Itoh, M. 152

Jessop, B. 180

Kaleckian theory 66
Keynes, J.M. 68, 118, 151
Keynesian theory 59, 66–7, 118, 151, 166
  post-Keynesian theory 66–8
King, J.E. 12, 101

Labour theory of value 9, 14–22, 24, *see also* labour, Marx's value theory
Labour
  abstract or social 18–23, 25, 29, 119
  average 155
  concrete 19–22, 29, 103, 119
  control 16, 23–4, 26, 42, 46, 49, 70, 80, 82–4, 119, 178
  double character v
  indirect 20
  intensity 42, 45

Labour *continued*
living 20, 39–40, 95, 97–8, 103–6, 120, 132–3, 161, 169
market 4, 20, 42, 81–2, 99, 176
necessary 39, 53, 103, 120, 131, 150
paid 6, 169
power 11, 22–4, 31, 33–4, 37–9, 43–4, 48, 52–3, 55, 58, 68, 70, 73–6, 80, 83, 92, 106, 113, 116, 137, 168
process 23, 42, 49, 81, 84, 99, 102, 105, 119, 170, 174
productive 36, 46–52, 120, 133, 137, 141
skilled 21, 45, 82, 98, 119, 140, 170
socially necessary 19–21, 37, 97, 103, 120, 131, 150
subordination or subsumption 81–2
surplus 39
time 8–9, 19, 20, 23, 29, 37–9, 45, 53, 68, 103
unpaid 133
unproductive 46–51
use value 23, 37
wage 28, 31, 46–7, 49, 76, 78–9, 176
see also capital, deskilling, division of labour, employment, labour markets, labour theory of value, productivity, skill, synchronisation, unemployment, value of labour power, versatility, work, workers, working day
Lapavitsas, C. 60, 101, 134, 152
Lapides, K. 73
Law 98, 110, 112, *see also* law of the tendency of the rate of profit to fall, tendency
Law of the tendency of the rate of profit to fall (LTRPF) 7, 89, 95, 102, 109–11, 133
LTRPF and counteracting tendencies 110–14
LTRPF and crisis 118–25
LTRPF and internal contradictions 114–18
Law of value 150
Lebowitz, M. 73, 181
Lenin, V.I. 87
Leopold, E. 73, 141
Levidow, L. 49, 180
Luxury goods 8

Machinery 21, 25, 27, 29, 33–4, 37, 40, 42–6, 53, 58, 81–2, 84, 91, 97, 105–6, 110, 130, 133, 144, *see also* instruments of labour, mechanisation
Macroeconomic policy 172
Malthusian doctrine 97–8
Manufacture 36, 48, 77, 120
Marginal efficiency of capital 151
Marglin, S. 87
Market exchanges 17, 19–20, 32, 53, 59, 65, 72, 75–6, 79, 87, 98
relations 16–21, 24, 26, 29, 83, 86, 119, 172, 177
see also credit system, labour market, stock market
Marx, K. *see specific topics,* e.g., capitalism, price, surplus value
Materialism 2–3, 5, 7, 28
McLellan, D. 12

Means of production 11, 21, 24, 34–6, 39, 52, 54–5, 58–9, 61–3, 75–7, 80, 83, 97–8, 103, 129, 133, 138, 176
Means of subsistence 80, *see also* needs, standard of living
Mechanisation 82, 84, 99, 112, *see also* machinery
Medio, A. 49
Merchant's capital 36, 56, 87, 135–41, 142–5
Method, Marxian 1–8, 10, 12–13, 14, 16, 21, 28, 64, 71, 155, 167–8, *see also* concepts
Milonakis, D. 101, 181
Mode of production 5–7, 10, 12, 15, 16, 22, 31, 39, 74, 77, 87, 99–100, 112, 154, 168, *see also* forces of production, production
Mohun, S. xi, 30, 50, 134
Money 16, 19, 24–5, 31–2, 34–7, 40, 51–7, 59, 62, 65, 67, 69, 75, 80, 93, 129, 131–2, 135–8, 140, 142–52, 173, 178
  as capital 34–6, 52–6, 60, 92, 135–6, 142–5, 148–50
  as money 52, 60, 135–6, 142, 144
  hoards 79, 143, 151
  means of circulation or exchange 52, 135
  means of payment 31–2, 35, 54, 145
  measure of value 31
  quantity 131
  standard of prices 31
  store of value 32
  value of 134
  see also credit, finance
Money-dealing capital (MDC) 136, 145–6
Monopoly 21, 91–2, 94
  means of production 11, 24, 34
  rent 162, 165
Moseley, F. 13

Nature 157, 164, 175, *see also* environment
Needs 8, 16, 34, 49, 77, 100, 179
Neoclassical economics 16, 21, 59, 66, 150, 153–4
Neo-Ricardianism see *Sraffian analyses*
Newton, Sir I. 111

Oakley, A. 12
Okishio, N. 111, 121–5
Overproduction 83, 90, 93, 95–6, 147, *see also* crisis

Perelman, M. 87, 101, 181
Philpin, C.H.E. 87
Pilling, G. 29
Policy
  economic 99, 171–3
  fiscal and monetary 67, 79, 148
Poor Law 77
Post-Keynesian theory *see* Keynesian theory
Postone, M. 30
Poverty 2, 28, 98, *see also* needs
Price 4, 9, 11, 14, 19–23, 25–9, 31, 39, 52–3, 56, 59, 65–6, 76, 85, 90, 92, 94, 102, 107, 118, 121–4, 131–4, 138, 142, 161–2, 166
  market 21, 94, 162
  of production, 85, 126–7, 129–31, 137–8, 161–4
  relative 22
  see also value

Primitive accumulation *see* accumulation of capital
Product 23–4, 16, 47, 75, 95, net 49
Production 24, 31–4, 37, 42, 46, 52–7, 59–60, 63, 66, 68–9, 84, 105–7, 110–11, 113–15, 117, 119–20, 126, 131–5, 139–40, 142–4, 150, 154, 157, 162, 174
  social process v, 8, 10, 15–18, 20–7, 29, 31, 39, 44–6, 48–9, 51, 56–8, 74, 77, 80–2, 86, 88, 91–2, 94–7, 99, 103–4, 175, 177–8
  see also capital, capitalism, division of labour, forces of production, mode of production, relations of production
Productivity growth 46, *see also* economic growth, labour
Profit v, 4, 6–8, 11, 20–1, 25–8, 31–2, 36–40, 42, 48–9, 57, 59, 85, 90, 94–5, 127, 129, 132–3, 142–3, 145, 150, 153, 178–9
  commercial 127
  industrial 133, 145
  rate 7, 83, 85, 89, 95, 110–12, 114–16, 118–24, 127, 129–30, 132–3, 137–8, 145, 149–51, 163–4
  see also law of the tendency of the rate of profit to fall, profitability, profit–wage ratio, surplus profit, surplus value
Profitability 26, 28, 41–3, 47, 49, 67–8, 85, 90–1, 94, 96–7, 100, 111, 118–19, 120–4, 150, 156, 158, 174, 177–8, *see also* profit
Proletariat, development 77, 86, 96–100, 167, 169
  dictatorship v,
  historical role 100, 169
Property, landed 78, 154–8, 161–2, 164–5
  relations 16, 24, 71, 143, 146, 154, 172, 176–8

Radice, H. 180
Raw materials 21, 24, 33, 40, 45–6, 58, 97, 103–6, 113, 130, 132–3, 174
Recession 100
Reification 26, *see* alienation
Relations of production 8, 10, 18–9, 21–2, 25–7, 31, 38, 47, 51, 53–4, 56, 75, 112, 119, 131, 175, 179
Rent v, 25, 27, 127, 133, 153–5, 164–5
  absolute 153, 160–3
  differential (DR1) 153, 155, 160–3
  differential (DR2) 153, 157–163
Reproduction, *see* economic reproduction
Reserve army 98; *see also* employment, unemployment
Reuten, G. 60, 125
Ricardo, D.
  theory of falling profit rate 114
  rent theory 153, 156, 164
  value theory 9, 29
Rosdolsky, R. 13, 48, 60, 125, 152
Rosenthal, J. 13
Rowthorn, B. 49, 134
Rubin, I.I. 50, 165

Saad-Filho, A. xvi, 12, 30, 48, 60, 73, 88, 108, 134, 152, 180
Saving 62, 75, 143
Savran, S. 50
Schwartz, J. 29
Scott, S. 12
Serfdom 6, 10–11, *see also* exploitation, feudalism, slavery
Shaikh, A. 101, 134
Slater, P. 49
Smith, A. 9, 16, 21
Smith, T. 13
Socialism *see* communism
Speculation 32, 57, 69, 91–2, 94, 99, 117, 145, 147, 150
Sraffian analyses 49, 111, 134
Standard of living 25, *see also* means of subsistence, needs
State 16, 71–3, 75–7, 79, 83, 99, 101, 143, 150, 167, 169–75, 177–8, 180
  intervention 44, 71, 76, 101, 118
Ste Croix, G. de 180
Steedman, I. 134
Stock market 20, 85–6
Supply *see* demand and supply
Surplus profit 156–61, 163–4, *see also* rent, surplus value
Surplus value 6, 46–7, 52–3, 62–3, 127, 137
  absolute 40–3, 45, 48, 69, 77, 81, 113
  accumulation 54, 57, 61, 91, 99
  forms v, 126–7, 137, 139, 143, 145–9, 153–5, 158, 162, 164, 172
  production 35–40, 46–9, 51, 53–8, 67–70, 91, 95–6, 99, 110, 115, 126–7, 129, 133, 135–7, 139, 145, 161
  and profit 36
  relative 43–5, 69, 82, 84, 106, 110, 113
  see also exploitation, profit, surplus profit

Technical change 8, 41, 43–4, 63, 69, 77, 83–5, 89, 92, 97, 99, 102, 104–7, 115–16, 123–5, 157, 163
  relationship 11, 38, 45, 49, 58, 66, 80, 88, 148, 153–4
  see also competition, technology
Technology 8, 19, 39, 46, 49, 53, 78, 81, 83–5, 92, 94, 98, 105, 107, 120, 123–4, 157–8, 160, *see also* technical change
Tendency 7, 83–5, 89, 93, 95–7, 103, 106–7, 110–12, 115, 117, 119, 123–4, 126–7, 136–7, 149, 151, 176, *see also* counter-tendency, contingency, law, trend
Tonak, A. 50
Transformation of values into prices, input values, Marx's procedure, 'problem', stages, *see also* distribution, equalities, normalisation condition, per cent form
Trend 117, *see also* law, tendency

Underconsumption 93–6, 101, *see also* crisis
Unemployment 27, 67, 92, 96, 98–100, 117, *see also* employment
Use value v, 16–17, 20, 32, 52, 65, 69, 132, 142, 174

Valorisation, *see also* value
Value of labour power 38, 43–4, 49, 73, 105, 116, 125, 169
Value v, 4, 6, 9, 11, 14–15, 17, 19–24, 26, 28–30, 32, 35, 40, 42, 48, 51, 56–7, 64–5, 69, 85, 95, 104–7, 110, 113, 119–23, 125, 129–33, 138, 155, 160–2, 172, 174
  creation or production 32, 36–42, 53–4, 56, 64–5, 115–16, 119, 126, 138, 140, 175
  market 156, 159–61
  redistribution 24, 51, 54, 56, 58, 68, 85, 126–7, 129, 133, 139, 175
  transfer 36–7, 129
  see also exchange value, labour, price, surplus value, use value

Wage
  rate 39, 41–3, 68, 81, 94, 96–8, 100, 112, 121–2, 124–5
  relation 4, 6, 10–11, 20, 23–4, 26, 28, 31, 33, 36–9, 42, 46–7, 49–50, 52–3, 62, 66, 68, 70, 76–81, 97, 113, 116, 118, 122, 133, 138, 140, 167, 169–70, 176
  see also capital, class, exploitation
Wajcman, J. 49
Wealth 78
Weeks, J. 30, 48, 73, 88, 101, 125, 152, 180
Wheen, F. 12
Wood, E.M. 13, 87, 180
Work 10, 23, 34, 40–2, 45–6, 58, 75, 81, 85, 140, 169, 172
  capacity 22, 75
  collective 81
  ethic 29
  exploitation 39, 47, 49, 68, 71–2
  extension 42
  intensity 41–2, 45
  see also labour
Workers 20, 23–6, 31, 33–4, 37–8, 40, 42, 44–5, 47, 49–50, 52, 61–2, 70, 75, 77–84, 89, 91, 93, 97–100, 107, 135, 140, 143, 155, 167, 169–170, 172, 177, 179
  capacity to labour 22
  exploitation 6, 116
  power 9
  productive 133
  unproductive 47
  see also labour, work
Working day 41–3, 70, 81, *see also* labour, work
Wright, J. 73

Young, R. 49